"Medicine became my vehicle to reach out and care for humankind."

Harry L. Graber, MD
Founder of Cardiology
at Mary Rutan Hospital
Bellefontaine, Ohio
Dec. 2016

THE MAKING OF A PHYSICIAN

THE MAKING OF A PHYSICIAN

---THIS WAS MY CALLING---

Harry L. Graber, M.D. F.A.C.C.

Library of Congress Control Number: 2016910386
ISBN: Hardcover   978-1-5245-1278-1
               Softcover   978-1-5245-1279-8
               eBook   978-1-5245-1280-4

Acknowledgement:
"St. Louis University Medical School"-cover artist, Clark Hulings
Elizabeth Hulings, Diamond Director
The Clark Hulings Fund for Visual Artists

Print information available on the last page.

Rev. date: 07/25/2016

To order additional copies of this book, contact:
Xlibris
1-888-795-4274
www.Xlibris.com
Orders@Xlibris.com
738634

CONTENTS

Because I was a non-thriving child until age two, my mother prayed to God that if He would spare me, she would dedicate me to Him. Not only did she pray for me on this one occasion, but also many times since then. Because of her unwavering love and support to me, I dedicate this book to my mother.

FOREWORD

My life's journey in medicine was put into writing by the urging of certain individuals who have become my coveted friends. It is my hope this story will enlighten and encourage others to also share their journey of life, whatever that may be.

In this book, the reader will encounter the importance of environmental experiences in life's decision-making. I have purposely included a few negative adventures of my early years to show how that also affects decision-making in a negative way. I also provided the secret how I was able to correct my early downward course of life—the result of which brought on a life-changing adventure of purpose and excitement in medicine.

It is my hope the reader will grasp the concept that medicine became the *vehicle* for me to reach out to people, not only to assist with physical healing but also to actually *care for the patient*.

Purpose Of The Book

There are several purposes for writing this book.

A main purpose is to serve as an autobiography. It gives insight into the author's life: how certain environmental experiences influenced him in making wise career choices. The book also illustrates how a young physician chose not to run away from a given community, because of an existing hospital of poor reputation, but instead to set out to help make the necessary positive changes—a healthcare institution that now has received national recognition. The third purpose in writing this book is to provide insight for the person who is contemplating career choices, especially the medical profession.

INTRODUCTION

Walking into the college snack bar to check my mail, I peeked into the student mailbox and pulled out a letter. I looked at the envelope and at first glance noticed it was from my favorite elementary education professor. I wondered, *What could this be about?* I quickly opened the letter. It wasn't very lengthy, and the only thing staring at my face was "I think God has something else for you to do than to become a teacher." Wow! What a dramatic forecast! It was near the end of my junior year of college, and everything was going great. I had just been elected as president of *Future Teachers of America* and was very focused upon becoming a teacher—now this! Just by reading the title of my book you assumed correctly—I changed my career to become a physician. But what transpired between those seven years? Why would I want to become a physician? The answer will be found in this book.

Ten physicians consented to briefly write their stories, answering the question "Why did you become a physician?" What they shared was quite interesting. They provided various stories, but in every instance, either an individual or an experience affected their lives, as well as their decision-making.

In this book, you will encounter over and over the importance of hereditary and environmental factors, with environment playing the greater role. The importance of this concept was introduced to me in the 1950s during my postgraduate studies in education at Indiana University. In a recent *National Geographic* article, an author described MRI evidence confirming children who live in a wholesome educational environment where parental love, quality music, educational toys, etc., are introduced enjoyed an increase in their IQ. It also suggested children who were deprived of a wholesome environment improved their IQ after positive initiatives were introduced. The poet Walt Whitman touched upon the importance of environmental factors in his poem "There Was a Child Went Forth." In it, he described that a child becomes a part of what he encounters for a day or a part of a day, or for many years or cycles of years. It is interesting that this environmental factor doesn't go away but becomes a part of who we are. Looking back into my early years on the farm, many of the valuable environmental experiences became incorporated into my genetic traits, such as putting work before play, never giving up, believing a job is not done until it's completed, having integrity, and caring for others, to name a few. Several premedical experiences that were a part of my early environment included placing splints on the broken legs of two baby lambs and detecting infected yellow spots (from *tularemia bacterium*) on the carcasses of certain wild animals. These and other stories are included in this book—special parts of my environmental encounters.

I hope my life story I shared in this book will motivate the reader to reflect upon their own environmental experiences and how they have affected their decision-making in life. For me, I understood the environmental factors of my life to be *providential*—for a divine purpose. Accepting this concept helped me to make the proper choices. Robert Frost, also a great American poet, said in his poem "The Road Not Taken," "I took the path less traveled by, and that has made all the difference." As you read this book and keep this quote in mind, you will discover that I, too, chose the path of life less traveled, and it has made all the difference for me. I would like to travel the path I had chosen, just one more time.

CHAPTER 1

Hereditary and Environmental Factors

As you learn about the genetics and environmental
traits of my family be thinking about yours as well
—especially environment!

Genetic Traits

As should be the case, only a brief part of this chapter will be focused
on genetics, just enough to highlight a few of the hereditary traits of the
Graber family. It will focus upon early environmental experiences that
occurred during the first eighteen years of my life while living at home in
rural Northeastern Indiana.

Most of the Graber ancestry exhibited competitive and inquisitive
traits. My early ancestor, Joseph Graber, was born in 1840 and lived in the
Alsace region of France. He was very inquisitive and innovative. He received
numerous medallion awards from several fairs for his genetic work with the
cross-breeding of cattle. He was the genuine founder of a breed specifically
suited for the Laurel mountainous region, called the *Montbeliard Breed*. He
was dubbed knight, then nominated officer of the Legion of Honor for his
agricultural qualities.

My grandfather, John Graber, was a slender-built man, measuring
nearly six feet in height. His wife, however, was short and of a stocky
frame. While my one brother was nearly six feet tall, I was only five foot,
six inches in height. While he was interested in mechanics and was less
athletic, I was interested in all sorts of athletics and enjoyed scholastics.

1

Joseph GRABER (1840-1923)

Joseph Graber (1840-1923)

My father was a very successful and ingenious individual. I do not believe there was anything he thought he could not do. He played organized baseball during his early years. He exhibited a variety of creative and competitive traits. Some proved to be invaluable as we lived through the Great Depression years. He spent multiple hours in his workshop making different items to be used on the farm. He made numerous pieces of furniture that were to be used inside our house. When electricity came through our community, he was quick to take advantage of the opportunity to install electric wiring in our house and farm buildings. He also installed the indoor plumbing for our new bathroom and kitchen. He was good at repairing things. Rarely did he throw anything away. He repaired our broken toys. He purchased old tricycles and repaired them to make them look and function like new. He also made a motor scooter for my brother and a motorbike for me. He was very creative!

My brother, Edwin Graber, was fifteen months older than me. We did a lot of things together in our free time. One winter, we spent weeks designing and creating a snowmobile mounted on three steel blades from old ice skates, to be used on ice. This was long before snowmobiles were in existence. A wooden frame was designed so as to have one steel runner in the front and

2

to be steered by a handlebar apparatus. The back of the structure was to have two stationary ice skate runners. A three-horsepower Briggs & Stratton engine was mounted onto the back of the wooden frame. On the engine shaft was fitted a large propeller that was designed and created by us. It was an attractive invention! After the snowmobile left the assembly line, it was ready for a stationary test run. As we started the gasoline engine the propeller began to turn, making a whiffing sound. It created a considerable air current. Everything worked just fine and we were quite excited. To further test our newly created invention, we thought we would rev up the rpm of the engine. When we did this, the entire shop vibrated, and the framed structure of the snowmobile began to weaken. Becoming quite frightened, we quickly stopped the engine. Unfortunately, the snowmobile never made it out of the workshop.

Although I was smaller than most boys my age, I never realized I was the little guy. I competed against the best. One time, when in gym class during my freshman year in high school, we were competing in what was called Indian wrestling. The activity included having two individuals lying on the floor in the supine position, with heads opposite to each other and arms interlocked. Each would raise the leg that was next to the opponent's, to a vertical position, touching the other's shoe on the count of one. This process would be repeated a second time. On the third count, the objective was to raise one's leg quickly, interlock it with the opponent's, and flip him into a backward somersault. Although being smaller than most of my classmates, quickness and determination enabled me to become the winner of that event. Creativity and a competitive spirit were common genetic traits within our family.

Environmental Traits

1. Location

I was born August 23, 1931, second youngest of seven children. We were raised on a one-hundred-acre farm in Northeast Indiana, located at what was known as the *County Line Road*. It was the road that the famous *Long Horn County Line Cheese* factory was located. This was also the line separating the north boundary of Allen County from the south boundary of DeKalb County. The city of Fort Wayne was a major city of Allen County, located about fifteen miles south of where we lived. About eight miles north of where we lived was the city of Auburn, Indiana. Just west of Auburn was the small town of Garrett, Indiana. It was there where I was hospitalized with an unknown illness at age fourteen, a medical problem I will refer to later.

The homestead property consisted of a beautiful landscape that included two elongated hills that were thought to have been Indian mounds. We spent many winter weekends, sledding and skiing down those hills. The skis were homemade. Some were made from barrel staves; others were made from long, thin, and narrow oak wood slabs that were highly polished, with the tips curved upwards. Several creeks ran through the farm property. There were three separate wooded areas on the farm. They included a mix of oak, hickory, maple, walnut, and wild cherry trees. One of the woods had a worn path meandering through it. It was an attractive setting. Although this was not the original site where my parents began their life together, it was the only place I knew. I loved it! It became my hunting and trapping grounds. It also became the place where I received my training for hard work and responsibility.

Birth Place of Dr. Harry Graber

2. My Heritage

My father's name was Benjamin. He was born in 1895 near Montgomery, Indiana. My mother's name was Anna. She was born in 1900 in Allen County, Indiana. They married in 1917 and were of *Anabaptist* descent. My father's parents were of the Amish faith. He left home at an early time of life, choosing not to join his parents' lifestyle. Leaving his Southern Indiana community, he wandered westward, spending several years in the state of Iowa, splitting rails for fencing. Later he moved to North Dakota and eventually settled down between Allen and Dekalb Counties in Northeastern Indiana. My father was a very determined person. Although he rarely verbalized his love to us children, he expressed it quite often by the many things he did and gave to each of us. Not only was he very caring to us, but he was also the same to many other needy persons within the community. My father taught us sound work ethic. It was always "work comes before play." He was also in charge of discipline. My parents worked as a team in this regard. If mother witnessed some bad behavior from any of us children, she reported it to my father, and when needed, discipline was delivered. Some of our misbehaviors may have sneaked by, but not too often. My father was in charge of giving us three boys our haircuts. Each time he would ask what kind of a haircut I wanted, one like a preacher, a doctor, or a Philadelphia lawyer. It was quite difficult to answer his question because they always seemed to turn out looking the same.

Benjamin Graber, father of author

My mother was an extremely kind and caring person, not only toward the immediate family but also to everyone she knew. She was a hard worker, not only caring for her seven children but was also in charge of operating a large garden and truck patch, mending the clothing for all of the family, and doing the weekly washing. She had a big assignment, but she did it well! I never heard her complain about her role as a spouse nor about her responsibilities as a mother. She was a great spiritual and faithful individual!

Anna Graber, mother of author

The Great Depression (1929–1931) was a difficult time, but it turned out to be a valuable learning experience for people living in the United States of America. Many people my family knew did not have much to live on. However, it brought family groups together, those of different faiths and cultural backgrounds. It was a time for sharing, and it had a positive spiritual impact on many families. People shared their assets, produce, and foods with one another. They also gathered together for social fun times. Although most families struggled, those living on farms had slight advantages, having access to milk from the cows, eggs from chicken hens, meat from farm animals, and produce from their gardens. My father told how he would hire men who were out of work to help him on the farm.

Their salary would be either a hog or some other type of produce. Everyone was taught to do with less. Every little boy I knew wore patched pants and went barefoot from late spring to mid-fall. Although I was quite young at the time of the Depression, its effects lingered on for several more years. All work assignments were taken seriously, and everyone was responsible for specific tasks. Unknowingly at the time, these experiences proved to be invaluable lessons for each us in later life.

3. Special Environmental Experiences of Proven Value for Later Life

Recalling a quote from Walt Whitman's poem "There Was a Child Went Forth," he stated that the first object that the child encountered, he became. It may have been for a part of a day, or for a certain part of a day, or it may have been for many years or certain cycles of years. The concept of that poem provides a tremendous truism! It holds a profound meaning and importance for each of our environmental experiences in life. "What one focuses upon, one becomes." The following paragraphs include several experiences of mine that influenced me to become the person I am and contributed to my becoming a physician later on in life. These experiences proved to be life-changing events for me.

Although the first experience occurred early in my life, my mother first told me the story when I was eighteen years old. She said that I was a nonthriving child from infancy to age two and was fearful I would die. She went on to say, she promised God that if He would spare me, she would dedicate me to Him. Needless to say, that story brought tears to my eyes.

The second experience represents environmental events that occurred during early farm life. It was natural for young boys like myself to observe how reproduction of mammals occurred from the beginning, through gestation and the giving birth. It was of interest and of importance to witness and participate with caring for the baby mammals that were born. It was also interesting to observe how my father and the veterinarian cared for the farm animals that required special medicine and attention during the time of their illnesses. Sometimes I witnessed failure of the special care that was provided, and the animal would die. Needless to say, I was all eyes and ears when I first encountered these special events.

The third environmental experience involved learning an important principle of "For every privilege there is an equal responsibility." My father gave me a calf when I was about nine years old. It was mine to keep, provided I assumed total care of it. As you might expect, the thrill of owning that calf would wax and wane when the responsibility end of the bargain got tough.

The fourth privilege was extra exciting. It consisted of a special gift from my grandfather. My grandfather called me one day and asked if I would like to take care of two baby lambs that were disowned by their mother. He stated that each of the little twin lambs had a broken leg and would need special care. I was excited! A little ingenuity was required for carrying out this experience. I used thickened cardboard strips with tape and splinted each of their broken legs. The legs healed nicely but remained slightly crooked. My grandfather taught me how to prepare a milk formula and demonstrated how to bottle-feed the lambs. The twin lambs became my special pets.

A fifth environmental experience began when I was five years old and continued through my second year of college. At age five, my father taught me how to live-trap muskrats from the creeks on the farm. We would check the traps early every morning. When we would get a muskrat, we would make certain it had died. Each night, we would dissect the pelt from the carcass. As I got older, during trapping season, I would scout our creeks to find where muskrats and mink might be located and set my traps. I became quite good with my trapping skills. I also became quite skillful dissecting the furry pelts from the carcasses. The experience provided me the opportunity to learn much about the anatomy of different fur-bearing animals. One special point of interest was I noticed some of the livers from the muskrats contained yellow spots. Later, during my training years in pathology, I learned these spots probably represented evidence of *tularemia*, a bacterial infection that invades different wild mammals. These stories and other early farm life experiences served as important environmental encounters of my life.

My next two environmental experiences occurred during my first fourteen years of life and probably played the most profoundly influential roles in my becoming a physician. The first experience occurred when I was eleven years old. It involved helping care for my eldest sister, who developed a mental illness. The incident occurred after she was out of high school and was employed in Fort Wayne, Indiana as a housemaid. The family was not involved with the incident, but while living there, she was sexually molested. The incident triggered a severe mental breakdown which she could not overcome. She developed *paranoid schizophrenia*, a form of psychosis. This was a time in medical history when there were no oral medications for the treatment of this type of illness. The only definitive treatment available was to institutionalize the patient and administer electric shock treatments. While awaiting special hospital care and treatment, my parents and physician had their hands full. My sister became quite violent at times, especially toward men. My parents observed that my presence brought about a noticeable calming effect to her mind. While awaiting admission into a mental institution, it became my assignment to spend much time with her. She particularly enjoyed the outdoors, so we would walk over the hills and valleys and through the paths of the woods of our farm. This became a routine activity for about three to four weeks. While it provided instantaneous therapy for my sister, it was a very stressful time for me. Missing those many days of school affected my academic school life for months to come. Only later would I be able to translate this experience as being a positive one toward my decision to become a physician.

At age fourteen, life took a critical, downward bend for me. Athletics always provided excitement for me. Although I did not participate in organized sports during my first two years of high school, I played on a church team quite regularly. Basketball and fast-pitch softball were my special attractions. It was not uncommon for me to run three miles to school to play intramural basketball before school started. One night our church youth played in an old gymnasium. It was not kept up very well. Several days later, I became ill with a high fever and a severe sore throat. This was followed by the development of a rash, arthritic joints and lower right abdominal pain. Our family physician hospitalized me at the *Sacred Heart Hospital* of Garrett, Indiana. There, I was taken to the operating room and had my appendix and a small section of the right distal ileum removed (the ileum is the last portion of the small intestine). Penicillin had just been approved for clinical use. So I was given intramuscular injections of the antibiotic in my buttocks every twelve hours for the next two weeks. I dreaded seeing the *Catholic Sisters* coming to my bedside with a syringe and long needle, looking for a site on my buttocks that had not been punctured. Apparently the penicillin was not helping me, and I continued to deteriorate. Our family physician told my parents he had done all he could do, and it would be up to God to heal me. That was when our community experienced their first *ecumenical* faith gathering, for the purpose of healing a critically ill fourteen-year-old boy who was told he would most likely die. United were Anabaptist, Presbyterian, and Catholic Christians performing an *anointing with oil* healing ceremony. Three weeks later, I was discharged from the hospital, on the road of recovery. I had missed the last three months of my sophomore year of high school. Although I did not need to repeat my sophomore year of school, my GPA suffered.

The last environmental experience to be shared during my early years of life was another very special one, one provided to me by my high school softball coach. It was springtime, near the end of my junior year of high school. I had finished my lunch and was practice-pitching a softball against the brick wall of the high school building. I glanced to my right and noticed the varsity coach walking toward me. He had a softball in his hand. Apparently he had been watching me practice pitching. He said in a rather low-pitched voice, "Here! Take this softball home and start practicing." That is all that was said, but did it ever make me feel good! He noticed me! Why was this so important? Having gone through multiple stressful and exasperating experiences during the past several years of my life had a negative impact upon on my super ego. I had perceived I was looked upon as "that sickly one." That single encounter from my coach provided me with a feeling of acceptance, a feeling I had not experienced for a long time.

I took the softball with me as the coach instructed. Now, at home, I was responsible for milking all our cows with the electric milking machines. As the cows were being milked (probably too long), I would practice my fastball pitching outside against the barn door. But first, let me describe the door. The door was painted red with nice white trim that included a twelve-inch diameter circle in the middle. It was a perfect target! Every night throughout the summer, weather permitting, I practiced my pitching against that door. It included my fast pitch, curveball, raise ball, drop ball, and my change-up pitch. I actually got pretty good.

Not long after, the high school coach approached me to become a member of the varsity softball team. I told him I would be interested but didn't think my father would permit me to play. Well, that was not a good enough answer for the coach. He came to our house to convince my father to allow me to become a part of the softball team. The discussion ended with the understanding that I would be allowed to play with the varsity softball team, but if there was farm work to be done, that came first. I was very excited! I could hardly believe my father gave in to the coach's wishes. By the beginning of my senior year of high school, I became the fastest pitcher on the team. We had an outstanding season and our team was tied for first place in the league. There was one final game left to play, and that was to be played on our home diamond. I was asked to be the starting pitcher, but as luck would have it, my father said I was needed to help on the farm that day to disc a thirty-acre field of ground. I was nearly heartbroken. I bargained that if I got the work done on time, would I be allowed to play? I got a positive response. That next morning, I was up at three o'clock and in the field with our International "H" tractor, tilling the soil full speed. I completed my task in good time and was ready to perform my duty as a pitcher. As our team went to the field, and as I went to the pitcher's mound, I glanced toward home plate. Who did I see but my father, sitting on the bleachers right behind home plate. What a privilege!

The game became a pitcher's duel. The score was 0–0 going into the ninth inning. The opposing pitcher was up to bat. Since most pitchers aren't the best hitters, I threw him a fast pitch, down the center of the plate. He swung at my first pitch and hit the ball for a home run. Needless to say, we lost that final game, 1–0.

I replayed that high school game in my mind multiple times, and it remains just as exciting for me today as it did when I was seventeen. What was so important about that positive athletic experience? I was given the privilege to return to excellent health and once again live a life of a normal person. The stigma of being that "sickly child" was now gone. My competitive spirit was rejuvenated. I expressed my thanks to the family of Coach Stanley Garman when I attended his funeral in 2012. During the memorial service, the invitation was given for people to share something special about coach Garman. I raised my hand. The pastor asked if I wished to use the microphone. I replied, "No, I just need a little space." I stood up and shared how Coach Garman helped me regain my confidence during my latter days of high school by asking me to become a pitcher for the high school varsity softball team. Then I demonstrated my famous pitch in front of all those people who were in attendance at the memorial service. I received an astounding ovation!

CHAPTER 2

Early Environmental Values Challenged by External Forces

As you read this chapter, briefly recall my preschool environment. Then notice the subtle social-behavioral changes that entered my life over the next twelve years—the environmental exposure captured my attention and became a part of me, some for brief periods of time and some became a part of me for great lengths of time—just as Walt Whitman the poet said. Fortunately, those early preschool environmental traits were not erased—they remained within me throughout my life.

The purpose of the first chapter was to illustrate some basic differences between the genetic and environmental make-up of an individual, plus to stress the importance of environment in the early developmental phase of my life. Several personal examples were shared how these experiences were believed to have influenced the future decision-making of the writer. This chapter includes some basic values of my family that became a part of me during my first five years of life. It also describes how learned values are challenged when introduced to new environmental experiences, sometimes changing or adding to what was previously learned. It is my intent to demonstrate how some of my early environmental principles were challenged when introduced to a new environment, later to be recaptured and incorporated into my belief system throughout my life.

While enrolled in a postgraduate course in guidance education at Indiana University, we were given a quote from the Catholic Church: "Give us a child for the first five years of life, and that child will not forget our teaching." Reflecting upon my own childhood experience, I believe the statement holds great truth. Fortunately, I cannot remember any negative moments of my life during my preschool years. I was loved and well cared for. Practical spiritual dimensions were deeply woven into my mind. A special blessing was always offered before we ate our food. When we didn't eat all the food from our plates, we were reminded of the hungry children across the globe. Following each morning's meal, my father would lead in a short devotional. Sometimes the prayers would get a little long. We were given simple work assignments early in life. "Work before play" was understood. If a work assignment was not done correctly, it had to be done over again. Sundays were set aside as a special day to worship God at church. In preparation for church, we were checked to make sure we were dressed appropriately with our hair combed and our ears, just to make sure they were clean. In Sunday school, we were taught special lessons from the Bible and sang songs. We learned the principle of tithing early in life. As one can tell, my preschool environment was quite structured and controlled. With the controlled environment I described, did it provide me with the adequate principles and experiences necessary for my next step in life? An answer will be provided at the close of this chapter.

Author attended Hopewell School for Grades 1-8

My First Eight Years of Formal Education

The first grade of school introduced me to another environment. I attended a one-room school for the first eight grades of my formal education. There were new rules and regulations I had to adhere to. This became an extended family yet different. It was a time for formal learning unlike I had experienced from my parents. I became acquainted and befriended new boys and girls, some from different backgrounds and beliefs. There were new opportunities and temptations I had to deal with. This was a time to test the principles I had learned from my parents.

The school I was about to enter was named "Hopewell School." It was located exactly one mile north from where my family lived. Although there were seven of us children in my family, we were almost like two families. Four of my siblings were much older than the three of us younger ones. My brother next to me was fifteen months older than me, and my sister was five years younger than me. Back in the early to late 1930s, there was no school bus to provide transportation. Except for extremely inclement weather, we walked one mile to and from school. If the weather became extremely bad, my father would take us to school by car. At about two thirds of the way to school, three neighbor children usually joined us on our walk. Each of us carried our lunch in a lunch pail made of tin alloy. It was not uncommon that we would hear the school bell ring, which meant we had fifteen minutes to be inside the school building or be counted tardy. We learned quite early in our experience that being habitually late to school could prove costly.

Some years later, I wrote a poem about us three little children walking to school, called "Memories."

> Many were the days, brother, sister, and I
> Walked to school together on a narrow pebbled road.
> We had the best fun, the truest fun
> Ever a child could hold.
> Under one arm were the books we held,
> Written by men of prestige.
> In the other were pails of wholesome foods,
> Supplying our bodies' needs.
> Along the way we would pass a lane.
> From its winding path came a shout;
> A neighbor boy calling us to a halt,
> Wanting to join us on our route.
> Our days of young were happy ones;

But never again will we see
Those three little souls down the pebbled road,
Walking so joyfully!
Memories are the most pleasant thing;
So vivid tells its stories of past,
That in this trance, I am wondering,
Will memories be memories that last?

Physical Structure and Activities of the School

The outside structure of the school was made of brick. Above the front entrance was a bell tower. The entire east wall of the building contained many windows. There were two dressing rooms for our coats and boots. The entire front of the classroom was lined with chalkboards made of slate. The teacher's desk was located in the front of the room, and on it lay a sizeable wooden paddle. To the right front was a piano. Also in front of the room, above the chalkboards, was an American flag. The room contained about eight long rows of desks of varying sizes with attached, hinged seats that could be folded upward. Beneath each desktop was an open drawer to store our books. On the desktop was an open hole to hold an ink bottle. In the back of the room, was a large "pot-bellied" wood-burning stove, and near it was a large wood box. In the back right corner of the room was a portable bookcase with three shelves that held encyclopedias and other books for educational reading. New books were exchanged on a monthly basis. Right in front of the teacher's desk was a large *recitation bench*. The bench was used for students to occupy when it became time for a certain class grade to share and interact with the teacher and to discuss the previous day's assignment.

There were eight grades in the school totaling about thirty students. The teacher was trained to teach all grades as well as serve as the janitor of the school. In addition to teaching the basic subjects, weekly music classes were conducted by a music teacher who circuited each of the nine schools of our district. At the beginning of each school year, the music teacher would have "tryouts" for each student. Those with the best voices were called "blue birds," the next best "yellow birds," and those with the least favorable voices were called "red birds."

On December 7, 1941, Pearl Harbor was attacked, triggering the beginning of World War II, which involved the United States of America. This brought on a special atmosphere of national patriotism. Many patriotic songs were learned at my school and are remembered by me to this day.

The Weekly Reader became part of our assignment every Friday. It kept us informed with the important happenings of the war.

What about the quality of education we received at our one-room school? Having been an elementary school teacher for five years, I believe the quality of education we received at that time was quite comparable to consolidated school systems. I believe it depended pretty much upon the quality of the teacher. A favorite expression of mine is "Show me an excited teacher and I will show you an excited classroom." I believe this to be a truism. For me, my experience at Hopewell school was above average. In addition to studying our own assignments, we had the privilege of listening in on what was being recited from grades ahead of us. Some of us were given special responsibilities helping children who needed assistance. This helped the ones who were providing the assistance to better understand the materials themselves. Provided all the school assignments were completed, students were permitted to sit with another classmate and participate in additional educational activities together. One of my favorite extracurricular activities was to memorize the *Morse code*.

Besides exhibiting the usual methods for learning, our teacher would allow us to participate in competitive educational activities such as spelling bees and solving mathematical equations. In math competition, we would be divided into two teams. The chalkboard was used for this event. The teacher would state a problem, and on the word "go," the assigned persons would compete to see who could arrive at the correct answer first. The teacher would keep score to see which team would win. Not only were these educational games fun, but they also helped us perform computations with speed. There was also much emphasis placed upon the memorization of poetry. I am still able to recite some of these poems verbatim. Most of these educational activities proved beneficial for the student's learning. Besides, it was fun.

Not all the educational efforts pertained to learning the basic three R's. We also participated in competitive sports. There were about eight or nine one-room schools in our district of Dekalb County of Indiana. There were several special extracurricular activities that were deemed important to each school as well as to the entire community. These activities or functions served as a vehicle to bring people of the community together. Softball was one very popular sport in our school district. Teams from each school were made up of boys and girls who wished to participate. While this included mostly the upper classes, I was privileged to play on our team as early as the third grade. Those who did not play became the school's cheering section. Extracurricular activities such as this brought about a sense of loyalty and pride for their school. It also enhanced the concept of competition and good sportsmanship.

Another extracurricular activity included performances in drama and music. These were well attended by most families of the community. One year I was chosen to be the music director. Without remembering, the teacher placed the director's wand in my right hand, forgetting I was left-handed. She was disappointed with my lack of skill until she realized the wand had been placed in the wrong hand.

Environmental Experiences—From High School to College Entrance

Following graduation from my first eight years of education in a rural setting, I was introduced to a new atmosphere and level of learning at a consolidated high school. While I was an excellent student during my first eight years of formal education, being transferred into a much larger school, with all new classmates, and being exposed to multiple teachers were quite overwhelming for me. It was an adjustment almost greater than I could handle. As a result, I felt lost and did not feel I belonged. Consequently, my grades plummeted. As luck would have it, those who befriended me were not persons who promoted a positive environment for good citizenship and learning. The fact that I was not allowed to participate in organized sports events added to my frustrations. Consequently, this was the beginning of a downspin in my life that remained with me until after my illness, which occurred during the last semester of my sophomore year of high school.

Shortly after graduation from high school, I was being recruited to enter Goshen College at Goshen, Indiana. After some days and weeks of private parental discussions, it was agreed for me to enter Goshen College in the fall of 1949. But as the summer went on, my father changed his mind. The issue was closed. Needless to say, this did not improve the relationship between my father and me. This added to a temporary breakdown of our relationship.

Not being able to go to college, I got a job at a grain elevator, where my father was employed. My work required stacking one-hundred-pound bags of feed supplement six and seven high. My other assignment was learning how to operate the gristmill. This meant feeding grain that was brought in by farmers into a grinder and mixing it with a special dietary supplement. This was dusty work but proved to be an excellent experience. It served as a good muscle builder, which in turn made me a much better softball pitcher. More importantly, it taught me how to interact with people of the community. It was also educational. It helped me learn a lot about the importance of providing good nutrition for livestock animals. My new job also provided me with responsibility, independence, management, and more.

With my monthly earnings, I was permitted to invest some of the money to buy a new car. With a new car, two things rated high on my agenda at this stage of my life, pitching softball and dating girls. I pitched a lot of softball for several teams in organized leagues that first post–high school summer. I also dated many girls. I dated one girl who was a professional roller skater. She took a serious liking to me and went along with me to ballgames and later to church. I was excited about the progression of this new independent life, but my father and mother were less thrilled. My dad realized he had made a mistake by not letting me enter college in the fall of 1949. As for my mother, she kept praying that her wayward son would soon make a change for the better. And I just kept on with what I was doing.

Two providential things entered into the picture. One, the same representative from Goshen College who had come to our home one year previously, returned. He wanted to know if my father had changed his mind. I was never told, but I think my father was hoping the college recruiter would show up again. This time it didn't require any "arm twisting," or lengthy discussions with my dad. He gave the gentleman an affirmative answer.

The second providential event occurred when my mother and I were picking pears. I was high up on a ladder picking pears when my mother began lecturing to me about the choices I was making in my life. She told me that she had dedicated me to God when I was an infant. She went on to explain that I was a nonthriving baby, and she was fearful I would die. So she prayed to God that if He would spare me, she would give me to Him. Well! I had never been told this! Why now? What could I do or say, standing high on a ladder and being lectured to like this? I never replied. Although I knew she was right, I experienced feelings of ambivalence inside, both anger and guilt. The topic was never brought up again. I carried that maternal lecture in my heart several more years before it was finally digested, and a positive change within me came to fruition. Not long afterward, I ended the relationship with that attractive girl on roller skates and entered Goshen College as a freshman in the fall of 1950.

Although I have not shared all my early environmental stories with you, enough has been told to make a valid statement or two. One, as I went forth, the environmental experiences of my early preschool years of life became a structured part of me, deeply woven into my innermost being. I was taught those basic rights from wrong, not only from within the home but also from the church community as well. I was also taught the important concept that privilege includes responsibility and work precedes play. I also experienced love, not only by words alone but also by the care that was given to me.

As my environmental experiences expanded to include the school, and surrounding community, my early learned value system became challenged. This is when conflict began to develop, especially between my father and me, lasting longer than it should have. Reflecting back upon some of those experiences, I believe every controlled guideline that was given was provided for my best interest and protection. However, in retrospect, I believe the path outlined for me to travel was too restrictive, causing me to rebel at an important phase of my early life. As a consequence, my educational learning suffered for the next couple of years. This being stated, I too shared some responsibility for the devious direction of life that I had chosen. About five years later, I wrote and mailed this "Prodigal Forgiveness" letter to my father:

> ### For all the pleasant times
>
> Spent together,
> In our work and play;
> From the earliest recollections,
> To the present,
> I would like to express
> A sincere "Thank you!"
>
> For all the clouded times
> Spent together,
> And whether it was you or me
> Whose thoughts were not interpreted
> As they ought,
> I ask a "Prodigal Forgiveness"
> from my father, whom I love.
>
> Amen.

The quote, supposedly made by the Catholic Church, reinforces my belief that those early environmental teachings of life, though disregarded for a while, remain within an individual for a lifetime.

Environmental Experiences of College—1950–1954

Free at last! At least this is what I thought. Somehow, for the first one and one-half years of college life, I seemed to have lost the important quote "For every privilege, there is an equal responsibility." But I didn't forget the privilege part, especially my first year of college. I exercised my privileges from morning to dawn. I became good friends of several of my classmates who were just as unsettled as me. Sports, especially fast-pitch softball, was quite high on my list. I became one of the top softball pitchers to beat, not only during my freshman year of school but also throughout all four years of college. We roomed in an old army barrack that had two side-by-side units attached together in front with a common entrance. The canvas drapes that served as petitions for two double bunk bed enclosures provided little privacy and definitely were not soundproof. Although we had steam heating, the outer walls were poorly insulated. But we had fun; actually, that was all we had—an abundance of fun. Although I did not sign up for a given roommate, I was assigned to be with a freshman whose first name was also Harry. He was about six feet two inches in height and of slender build. He walked with a long, slow stride and spoke with a slow drawl. I was only five foot six inches in height. We became very good friends and were soon known on campus as *Mutt and Jeff.* We were well liked by a lot of the student body. Although we appeared studious, studying was not our major objective. I had an attractive brown leather-bound carrying case that my mother had given me for college. It contained all my books, and I carried it wherever I went. I looked quite impressive! One day, that brown leather-bound carrying case got lost. To make things worse, all my books were in it. How could I study without my books? Three days went by before the carrying case was found. Somebody played a trick on me and hid it in the girl's restroom of the gymnasium.

I will share one more hilarious experience of mine, only to point out what happens when one loses focus of purposeful living and accountability. You have heard the saying "No work and all play makes Johnny (in this case, Harry) a dull boy." That is exactly what happened to me. During my freshman year of college, all students were required to take the course "Introduction to Psychology." No, I didn't lose my briefcase again, but I did lose my direction in life for a short period of time. I don't remember whether I ever read that textbook of psychology, but on the final exam, I earned a D-. I was privileged to repeat the test, and this time I received an F. I can still hear the loud laughter among my army barrack friends. Well, the laughter didn't last too long, because it wasn't long before my parents received the results of my failing grade in psychology. Needless to say, their knowledge of my failing grade provided me with a purposeful stimulus and positive change in my life.

I learned quickly that if I wanted to enjoy the *privilege* of staying in school, the other part of the equation must be taken seriously, and that was *responsibility!* I became serious about making a positive change in my life. It was during the early part of the second semester of my sophomore year of college that I developed a severe laryngitis, losing my voice for nearly one month. Academically, I was doing much better, but not being able to talk proved to be a big handicap for my learning. I had been seeing a physician about my throat problem but was not improving physically. I remember the doctor saying that my throat looked normal, and was asked how I was doing spiritually. I caught on to the direction the physician was leading me. You know how on a computer, one can tap a certain icon, and it brings about many bits of information of a given topic. Well, that physician tapped an icon in my brain that opened up certain early mistakes in life that I was responsible for, mistakes that needed correcting. You guessed it—I quickly made right those specific matters involving the people, and God, whom I had wronged. This was the beginning of an important turnaround of my life at large, as well as my academics at college. Grades improved immensely.

I was doing quite well in all my studies, and by the end of my sophomore year of college, I was declared a major in elementary education. I was elected president of *Future Teachers of America.* I was also able to continue with my athletic activities as before, without interfering with my studies. More importantly, I was excited with the choice of elementary education as my major.

It was near the close of my junior year of college when I received another monumental surprise. Every year, the school had a week of formal spiritual renewal services. Although not a requirement to attend, I decided to attend one session. The speaker was a returning missionary from India. I recall that the service was quite impressive, and I was spiritually moved to make a deeper commitment to my Heavenly Father and his Son, Jesus Christ. Although I had been baptized at age eleven, the true conversion experience of my life occurred during the latter part of my junior year of college. About two days following these special services, I received a letter from a faculty member, Dr. Mary Royer, my favorite elementary education professor. In it she wrote, "I think God has something else for you, than becoming a schoolteacher." This was quite shocking information, to say the least. At this point in my life, I was quite excited about becoming a teacher. I filed this information in my brain and continued with my major in education.

It was near the close of my senior year of college, and I was making applications to different schools for a teaching position. I was still single and quite satisfied with the direction I was traveling in life. One day, while browsing the bulletin board in the administration building, I noticed a note—"Wanted! Seeking teachers for the Navajo Indian Reservation"— signed by the chief of the Bureau of Indian Affairs. I was excited! I immediately returned a letter to the bureau and received a written response from the chief in ten days. The letter included an application and an essay test to be completed by me. I finished the written requirements and returned it to the proper address. Shortly afterward, I learned that I was accepted.

In conclusion: Although I temporarily deviated from some of the early environmental values I learned from my parents, teachers, church community, and community at large, these values didn't escape me permanently. Many of those important principles helped me to become the person I am today. Before going on to the next chapter, reflect upon your life's journey, and consider how certain early environmental experiences influenced you in choosing your path of life.

CHAPTER 3

Early Teaching Experiences

In this chapter, the reader will sense my excitement as a teacher, working with the Navajo children. But at the same time, a question begins to surface. "I think God has something for you to do, other than teaching," as told by my former professor at Goshen College.

My college days were now over. I had just marched through the graduating line to receive my diploma from Goshen College. Within the sheepskin-covered diploma was the important certificate that said "Bachelor of Science Degree in Education." This was an important stepping stone in my life, and I will always remember those individuals who helped reshape it. I was now ready to experience another exciting phase of my environmental journey, teaching Navajo children at a boarding school in Tuba City, Arizona. I hurried to pack all my accumulated belongings from my years spent at Goshen College, and then start home to spend a few days with my parents before traveling westward. Four years of college environment provided many opportunities of both spiritual and educational growth, yet this was just the beginning of what God had in store for me.

Arizona, Here I Come

After my 1950 Plymouth sedan was completely packed with all my clothes and educational belongings, I kissed my parents good-bye and started toward the state of Arizona, a destination of nearly 1,850 miles. Upon entering St. Louis, Missouri, I traveled on U.S. Highway 66 until I arrived at Flagstaff, Arizona. As you may or may not know, U.S. 66 was also known as the "Will Rogers Highway," and also the "Main Street of America." It began at Chicago and went all the way to Los Angeles, California. It was one of the original highways within the U.S. highway system. After passing through Albuquerque, New Mexico, I soon came to Gallup, New Mexico. Gallup is about twenty miles from the Arizona stateline. It is known as the "Indian capital of the world." It is one of the oldest and largest Native American gatherings in existence and is where they gather to hold their Inter-Tribal Indian Ceremonials each August.

As I approached the Arizona state line, I began seeing a few Native Americans either walking along the highway or sitting alongside the road attending to their booths, selling collectible jewelry, etc. As I passed by these areas, I could feel my heart beat from excitement. Although I still had over two hundred miles to travel to meet my destination, time seemed to pass quickly. This was new territory for me. When I was about fifty miles from Flagstaff, Arizona, I noticed some beautiful mountainous peaks. As I got closer, I could identify the "San Francisco Mountains." There was still a small amount of snow capping the peaks.

I finally arrived at Flagstaff, made a right turn onto U.S. 89, and headed toward Tuba City, Arizona, which meant I had about ninety more miles to reach my destination. One and one-half hours later, I saw a small white-painted sign, which read "Tuba City," eleven miles to the right. My adrenalin level was high by this time. The trip was nearly completed, the traveling part, that is. During the last eleven-mile stretch, I saw nothing but tan sand, sprinkled with occasional olive-colored sage bushes, and attractive rock formations, some stretching above the mesas. I even noticed several petrified logs. I was so busy watching the different rock and sand formations that I paid little attention to the extreme roughness of the sharp pebbled road. This part of my journey was completed. I arrived at Tuba City, Arizona!

The Village of Tuba City

Tuba City appeared as a small village. The first main attraction was the trading post. Standing in front of it were several Navajo Native Americans, clothed in their typical attire. Turning left onto the main drag were rows of trees lining each side of the sand-covered street. On the right side was a Presbyterian church, and to the left I saw multiple large rust-colored brick buildings with a sign that read "Tuba City Boarding School." There were other buildings too, but I did not know what they were being used for. Farther down the street stood an elongated, one-story building. There was a sign that read "Hospital." Beyond the hospital were many more small house dwellings. To the left of me were people going into a building. I parked my car and went into the same building to ask for instructions. I was directed toward the administration building to report to the administrative clerk, who accompanied me to my temporary housing quarters. The following day, I was introduced to the school superintendent, my principal, and fellow teachers. Since this was early summer, all the boarding school children had been dismissed to return to their parents. All the teachers were cleaning up their classrooms and attending special educational meetings to prepare for the following school year. I was given a special library assignment to code all the new books that had been purchased, using the Dewey Decimal System.

The Native American Navajo Tribe and the Land They Possess

Although my main objective will be to share my environmental experiences among the Navajo people, it should prove helpful to know a few fundamental facts about the people and the size of the land they possess. My comments will relate to what I observed to be true when I lived there in the mid-1950s.

The Navajo people are very family oriented. They are a spiritual people. The population is about 250,000. The geographical size of the Navajo Nation covers nearly 27,425 square miles, about the size of West Virginia. It includes the southeastern part of the state of Utah, northeast portion of Arizona, and the western part of New Mexico. The land is semiarid, and many parts are sandy. There are numerous mesas or plateaus on the reservation, with an occasional spring-fed oasis. Several of the mesas are owned and occupied by the Hopi Indian Tribe. The elevation for most of the reservation exceeds five thousand to six thousand feet above sea level. On the reservation are caverns, canyons, and an abundance of uranium ore. The rainy season occurs during the late summer months.

There are significant health issues among the Navajos, including diabetes, alcohol abuse, obesity, and a genetic disease causing an immune deficiency. There is an increased incidence of cancer noted since the beginning of uranium mining, particularly involving the productive organs of young females.

The Navajo people retain the largest land area than any other U.S. tribe. They have one of the largest tribal governments of all other North American tribes. They have their own law enforcement and social systems. Because jobs are not readily available on the reservation, unemployment is high. Many men have to seek employment outside their reservation. There are still a significant number of sheep and cattle grazers.

As with all Native Americans, certain ceremonial events play an important part of their social and spiritual lives. One very important event occurs every summer during late August. Native American tribes gather from all parts of the United States and Canada and some from Mexico to meet at Gallop, New Mexico, for various events, including rodeo competition and tribal dancing. There are numerous Christian mission groups established over the Navajo and Hopi reservations, of which the native people have become an active part.

During the 1950s, most of the Navajo children attended boarding schools. This was true when I spent my first year at Tuba City. I recall traveling with busloads of children to different states. The children would be separated from their homes for months at a time. Now, most attend public day schools or church schools located in or near their own communities.

Many changes have occurred since I lived on the Navajo Reservation during the mid-1950s. When I revisited Tuba City and other parts of the reservation in 2012, I took note of some of these changes. There were restaurants, paved roads, motels, new public schools, modern hospitals, and automobiles, to name a few. The old trading post at Tuba City was entirely modernized and converted into a commercial store.

The rest of my story, while working with the Native American Navajo children, will be how I was affected by this invaluable experience and how certain people helped to shape my early life in pointing me in the direction of medicine.

My Assignments

The first of my two-year assignments at Tuba City Boarding School included (1) recruiting Navajo children for enrollment into the local boarding school at Tuba City, (2) teaching a third-grade class, (3) serving as librarian, and (4) serving as assistant scoutmaster for the Boy Scouts of America.

Soon after my arrival, I was given the assignment to check all the books of the school library to make sure all were coded correctly according to the *Dewey Decimal System*. In addition, I was asked to accompany a Navajo scoutmaster to try to recruit students for the upcoming school year at the Tuba City Boarding School. Although the Arizona state law required all schoolchildren to attend school, there was no enforcement of the law on the reservation. Our task was to try to persuade the parents to let their children attend the boarding school. The scoutmaster was very impressive. Although he spoke excellent English, he had a very persuasive way of convincing the parents in Navajo language to enroll their children in school. We canvassed a very large territory. It was difficult to describe the distance we covered. But it was said that the South Rim of the Grand Canyon was about fifty miles west of Tuba City, "the way the crow flies" where we entered into the base of the canyon to recruit prospective school children. This was a very interesting introduction for me to visit different families in their *hogans* (houses). Through special experiences like this, I later was privileged to attend several *ceremonial dances* and eat *fry bread and mutton stew* (the meat from sheep). One day, on our "scouting mission," the scoutmaster suddenly stopped the pickup truck, got out, and began looking onto the sand. When asked, he said he saw some deer tracks. Impressive!

The Boy Scouts of America organization was very interesting for me to participate in. I became an assistant scoutmaster. Besides our regular scout meetings, we would plan special outings, mostly in the foothills of the great Kaibab Forest. This would include an overnight stay in tents, with a "cookout." One outing included cutting Christmas trees to sell to the people of Tuba City and Moencopi (Hopi Indian Village). The main assignment of my first year was teaching a third-grade class at Tuba City Boarding School.

In the Classroom

The third-grade class was made up entirely of Navajo children, with ages ranging from nine to fifteen. Although the textbooks were from the Scott-Foresman Publishing Company, a lot of ingenuity was required to adapt the educational material to fit the Navajo cultural background. Besides the awareness of the cultural factor, there was a significant age spread within the class. Most of the boys and girls had never been off the reservation. The closest metropolitan city was Flagstaff, Arizona, which was ninety miles away. Most of the children had never seen or been inside a passenger train. Their environment consisted of living in a hogan with their family and helping to shepherd flocks of sheep. The only soil they knew consisted of sand. They had a deep appreciation of nature. Navajo people are very good observers and artists. Nearly all are masterful landscape artists. The children were very intelligent. The main thing they lacked was opportunity.

To provide learning beyond the basics of reading, writing, spelling, and arithmetic, I tried to get my students excited beyond their native environment. Those who had completed their lesson assignments were permitted to sit at a special reading corner to read books. In science, I would try to provide learning experiences that incorporated their immediate surroundings and expand upon it. For example, we looked at the problem of erosion occurring in their land and talked about what could be done to help to prevent it from happening. After going out and viewing an eroded area, we created an "in-class model project" demonstrating evidence of erosion following a heavy rain. For this, we constructed a sizable box, filled it with soil, and tilted the box so that when filling a can with water and letting it slowly flow onto the sandy soil, it would cause a "wash-out." Then we created a similar model but planted the slope with grass. The children witnessed that the soil with the planted grass helped eliminate soil erosion—an excellent "hands on" learning experience. A second learning experience pertained to social studies. I had my class draw a large map of the entire United States . . . remember, they are very good artists. This project was to help each child experience some things beyond their present environment. After the map was drawn, they were to include all the states of the United States and their capital cities. Lastly, they were to include the major mountainous areas and the Great Lakes. After the map drawing was completed, each child was given an address of a person from a selected state, asking for a sample of soil to be sent back; students described the purpose of the need for the samples in their letters. After receiving the soil from the sender, one sample was placed in a small test tube and pasted onto the appropriate place of the map from which it came. The rest of the sample was used for planting their seeds. The purpose was to observe the different colors and texture of the soil samples and to see which soils produced better growth of their seeds. You cannot imagine how excited these children were when they received their small packages of soil, the process of planting the seeds, and to observe their growth.

This project proved to be a very exciting and important learning experience for the children. Multiple things were learned . . . not only social studies but also the language arts (letter writing), scientific experimentation, topography of the land, and the Great Lakes of the United States. A third highlight for this third-grade class was to take a field trip to Flagstaff, Arizona, and tour the inside of a passenger train. None of these children had ever been privileged to see or enter inside a passenger train. These learning experiences took this third-grade class far beyond the walls of the classroom and their native environment, and my environment became broadened as well.

Being a teacher at the Tuba City Boarding School in 1954–1955 proved to be a very valuable and exciting experience for me as well as my third-grade children. It had a social impact upon all of us. We became good friends. I don't recall having to deal with any social or discipline problems in that class. Every child was eager to learn. At the close of the school year, the children and I were given a special farewell picnic. There were a lot of sad faces at that picnic, knowing we would not be seeing each other again. One girl asked if she could go home with me. The same girl, on another occasion, asked if I belonged to the "white man." That was an interesting question. I doubt that she consciously noted the difference until someone told her. This was an exciting teaching experience for me! I loved my work. My principal liked my efforts too. She gave me an outstanding rating.

Second Year of Teaching—Assigned to Introduce a Day School Program

In my second year of teaching, I was given the assignment of principal/teacher—not a monetary promotion but one of increased responsibility. This was the beginning of a transition for the governmental school system. They began to establish a number of *day schools* on the Navajo Reservation so children would not have to be removed from their families (up to this time, many children would be transported miles from home to attend boarding schools). There were two day schools in the area where I was located. A day school compound consisted of two mobile trailers—one for a Navajo cook, one for the principle/teacher, and a quadrangular metal building for the classroom. The construction compound was always located near a windmill-driven well for water supply. In addition to being the teacher, the job included attracting parents to send their children to the day school. Another minor assignment was to serve as the maintenance man. A third gesture, though not included in the contractual agreement, was to provide emergency services for those who needed fast transportation to a hospital. For the first two assignments, it meant that I was required to be dressed in a sport coat, shirt, and tie plus carry several small tools in my pocket should the need occur to provide small maintenance work.

As was the case at Tuba City, the students who were to attend school might have ages ranging from five to fourteen. In this setting, they would all be considered as beginners, that is, teaching them some basic English words and phrases to prepare them for reading readiness by the end of the school year. One unusual governmental rule required "a timeout rest period" during each midday. Can you imagine students whose ages ranged from five to fourteen years, all lying on the floor for one-half hour each day for a rest break? The cook's duties were to provide a warm meal each day and to function as an interpreter for the students. The most difficult problem was, how does one go about teaching a foreign language (English) to a group of Navajo children? I was not given a curriculum guide or books to accomplish the reading readiness goal. Ingenuity was the key! Fortunately, I had access to lots of magazines and such to clip out pictures. So I would use these pictures, along with different objects that were available (fruits, vegetables, forks, knives, spoons, etc.) as objects to teach English words and phrases. For example, I would show the students a picture or object and slowly say the word, then say, "Den neh," meaning repeat after me. The cook would be in the classroom with me to assist, by speaking to the children first in Navajo language and then in English. It was somewhat simplistic but proved successful. I spent two months of the second year at the Cow Springs Day School and then was transferred to Copper Mine Day School to complete an assignment for another teacher who left his post because of failure to recruit students.

As I mentioned, the first effort in starting a day school at Copper Mine proved unsuccessful. I had learned that to have a successful start in difficult projects often meant staying in the background and allowing someone who's familiar and popular with the people to "step up to the plate" and lead. My Navajo cook was Mrs. Sloan. She was educated, intelligent, and very cooperative to work with. Because the first effort to attract students to this school proved unsuccessful, Mrs. Sloan and I spent some time planning how we might attract the people of this community to take an interest in having their children attend the Copper Mine Day School. After much soul-searching, Mrs. Sloan came up with a very brilliant idea. The time of the season was near Thanksgiving, or what the Navajos called "Little Christmas." The plan was to provide a large meal, including "mutton stew" and "fry bread" with jelly, then provide a game of "tug of war." The event was advertised at the nearby trading post. On the day of the event, we gathered almost everyone from the community. Mrs. Sloan asked a blessing for the food and began serving all the people. After the meal, everyone participated in a vigorous tug of war. It turned out to be a great, eventful day! It was a tremendous success!

Children began coming to the school regularly, fourteen in all, ages ranging from five to fourteen. The method for teaching the English language was the same here, as it was at Cow Springs. The students were fast learners. Much gratitude was to be given to my excellent cook. She was absolutely great! I tried to locate Mrs. Sloan in 2012 but was told she had moved somewhere to the state of Utah.

Duties Were More Than Being a Teacher

Teaching was not the only duty for a day-school teacher. The teacher was to become part of the Navajo community. Sometimes it meant providing service to members of the community who might need emergency transportation to the hospital. It might also include transporting people to a special ceremonial dance gathering. I recall three specific emergency calls I was asked to make while at the day schools. It's interesting that all three of them occurred at night.

The first emergency call had to do with a term-pregnancy lady who was bleeding profusely. Looking back at the incident, this most likely represented an *abruption* placentae, where there is a premature detachment of the placenta, causing severe bleeding. I never did hear the final result of this emergency problem, but I hope both the mother and baby survived.

The second and third emergency occurred while I was located at the Copper Mine Day School. Again, both of these emergencies were at night, occurring two weeks apart; both involved the same baby. Copper Mine was located about fifty miles, slightly west and then north of Tuba City, the village where the hospital was located. At the time of the first emergency run, the father of the baby was told that the child was all right. Two weeknights later, I heard a knock on my trailer door. It was my Navajo cook. She said, "The baby is sick, again, and needs to go to the hospital." I was quite puzzled by this request, because two weeks ago I had been told the baby was all right. I told my cook to relay to the father that I would first need to go to the trading post to get gasoline. I also told my cook to ask the father if he would help pay for the gasoline, because I had very little money in my wallet. Well, he consented, and I went to get gasoline for my car, which happened to be opposite the direction of where I needed to go to pick up the sick child. Unfortunately, this took quite some time until I was able to reach the father's hogan. After I did arrive at the home, I was met by a couple of Navajo people, one of whom was an elderly man. Remember, it was night, and all I could see were lights flickering in the distance. The man tried to communicate with me in his native language, none of which I understood. After failing to understand, he went after another lady to speak to me. This happened to be one of the parents of a student of mine. She spoke English fluently enough that I could understand her. She told me to go home, that the baby was not sick. I was quite puzzled with her comment. I didn't know if the family was upset for asking to help pay for gasoline for my car, or what the reason might be. But I listened to her advice and started for home. The next day, my Navajo cook told me that the baby had died, and I was not needed for the ceremonial. Needless to say, I felt very saddened about the death of this little child. I wrote a short poem about this event. It probably makes little sense to anyone but me. At the time, I felt the death seemed so cruel and unnecessary, so I penned this short verse.

> Death at the Hogan
> Austerely aroused by thoughts,
> Deeply engrained in solitude;
> Embedded with sorrow.
> Death has bombarded
> Someone's profile with unknown cause.
> No reason given.
> Caught by a mysterious destruction,
> Into an abyss, not understood
> By any human mortal.
> Only death and her captors
> Can describe the horror of it.
> Who shall be next to ask her?
> Prepare, oh fragile one,
> Lest by night
> You, too, might be captured!

Living Alone in the Dessert

Living alone in isolated and unfamiliar surroundings, among a people with customs and language that were poorly understood by me at the time, it was quite easy to misinterpret outside noises at night, or during the day for that matter. One day, a father of one of my favorite pupils came walking toward me with an unstable gait. I did not understand what he was saying, but I knew he was angry. I quickly went into my car and locked the door. Fortunately, my Navajo cook intervened. I didn't know what she said, but whatever it was brought on dramatic results. Soon, the man turned around and headed for his home.

Nighttime was even more spooky. One night, two men knocked on my trailer door. They were Caucasian men and neatly dressed. They introduced themselves as Mormon missionaries. I invited them into my trailer and listened to their spiritual presentation, then thanked them for coming to visit me.

It was not always people who came to my trailer by night. Other noises would get my attention too. One early wintry evening, I was aroused by the wind. As I went outdoors, I could tell a winter storm was moving my direction. Dead tumbleweeds were blowing eastward. The top branches of the rabbit and sage bushes were bent over because of the wind. I noted a black raven stopping its flight, either to rest or get some food. The snow began coming down at a forty-five-degree angle. I found this to be a very exciting occasion. I watched the developing storm for a while and then went back inside my house trailer. The next day I penned my exciting thoughts.

A Winter Invasion

In yonder, the autumn hill was quiet
And still, sleeping her time away.
But last night she was struck
By invisible arms,
Led by the cruel, Winter Wind.

In the valley below, someone was dancing;
Dancing in tempo with the wind.
Awkwardly moving
Was Rabbit Bush Yellow,
Deeply rooted in the winter scene.

Black Top Raven suddenly landed
To catch his second breath.
He sharpened his weapon
And amassed up with fuel;
Then quickly he flew again.

Busy little Pack Rat went hopping along,
Dragging his bedding behind.
There's not much time for leisure;
He must transit while he can.
He, too, was caught by surprise.

Everything is moving again!
Moving with haste!
Rushing opposite west!
Another invasion appears quite evident.
Banefully marching, is Old Winter Wind.

One other night I walked outside my mobile house to see what I could view. The night was extremely quiet. In addition to the sky, I was deeply impressed by the stillness and darkness of this particular night. As I looked up into the sky, never before had I seen so much activity and excitement. I never witnessed so many moving streaks of light produced by the passage of meteors than I did on this particular night. The moon appeared large and was shining so brightly. I believe every star was in attendance, ready to entertain me with a performance like I had never witnessed before. It was a creation of exquisite beauty, one I shall never forget! After carefully watching this panoramic view, I became deeply impressed, and my thoughts were directed toward the Heavenly Father. He seemed to have designed this moment of beauty just for me.

Our Guardian

Last night I saw the Earth
All peaceful and at rest.
In order not to awaken her
I toed my very best.

The Earth was well protected
By the Father up above.
Not once was it molested,
But guarded with His love.

The moon served as lighthouse;
The clouds as mounted forts.
The stars were sending codes
Out from their various ports.

I stood in reverence for a while,
Then kissed the Earthly Sea.
Having full assurance,
God watches over you and me.

Solitude, especially when privileged to be in a semiarid environment, provided me with the best of opportunities for reflection and meditation with my Creator and me alone.

The Beginning of Unrest

Reflecting upon my first year of teaching those third-grade boys and girls on the Navajo Reservation, I was well aware that this was an extraordinary privilege for me. I remained excited and quite satisfied that I had chosen elementary education as my major. So much so I requested to spend the first summer attending a postgraduate education program. I was given permission and was accepted to begin my master's study in guidance education at Indiana University. It proved to be time well spent and reinforced my belief that I had chosen the right profession.

But out of somewhere, unbeknown by me at the time, a former statement reentered from the subconscious to the conscious level of my brain, saying, *I think God has something for you to do other than teaching.* At the time, I wondered, *What is going on?* But deep within me, I knew. This became the beginning of my reflecting upon past environmental experiences, including the special people who had left their imprints upon my life. I have already mentioned those from my early childhood education days. I must now include certain people and other recent experiences I had encountered during my two years spent on the Navajo Reservation as a teacher.

There were several people who attracted my attention while living on the Navajo Reservation. One was Mr. Newsome, an African American gentleman who also taught at Tuba City, Arizona. He was there at about the same time frame as me. His life's goal was to enter law school to become an attorney. He was a very gentle, kind, and brilliant man. I could tell he too had a good upbringing. In his free time, he would always be reading. One of his favorite journals was the *Atlantic Monthly*, a magazine for the scholarly. I was much impressed! He loaned a copy for me to read, and to my surprise, I found myself utilizing the dictionary frequently, looking up words of unknown meaning to me. This was the beginning of my deep desire to become informed outside of my comfort zone. We revisited together one time after he had returned to Chicago and I had moved to South Bend, Indiana, to become a teacher in that school system. I would give anything to renew my acquaintance with this gentleman.

Another person was Donald Minter, MD. He was an employee at the local hospital of Tuba City, Arizona. His specialty was internal medicine. He and his wife befriended me. Both were such gracious and delightful people. His caring mannerism and soft-spoken voice left an indelible imprint upon me. He, too, became my lifelong mentor.

Reflecting back upon the many experiences I enjoyed while at Tuba City and Copper Mine, Arizona, two important memories stand out in my early life's journey. I observed pleasant but underprivileged people who were in need of better education, opportunities for employment, and a better system for receiving quality health care. These were my observations during the mid-1950s. Although my revisit in 2012 showed evidence of much improvement in those categories, my earlier observations of Native American life on the Navajo Reservation contributed much to my decision-making that eventually led me to the profession of medicine.

From Tuba City to South Bend, Indiana

At the close of my second year of teaching at the Navajo Reservation, a former Goshen College classmate asked me to consider applying for a teaching position within the same school system he was teaching, at South Bend, Indiana. He indicated there were openings for teachers. Still being single, I thought the idea sounded exciting. Besides, I could be near my college friend. I submitted a letter to the superintendent of the School City of South Bend, Indiana, expressing my interest in applying for a teaching assignment at the elementary grade level. I received a reply by letter, indicating there was an opening for a position at the Studebaker Elementary School. He suggested that if I was interested, I should fill out the application that was included in the reply letter. Thanks to my friend's influence, I was accepted. So I had an exciting and an important transition to make. Shortly after, I also received a call from an outreach organization of my church, asking if I would be interested in volunteering at a summer camp for crippled children. It didn't take too long to give them an affirmative answer. This provided me with something purposeful to do during the summer before moving to South Bend, but it also provided an opportunity to work with physically handicapped children.

The camp for crippled children was located in the state of Maryland, near Chesapeake Bay. The director and owner of the camp was a very prestigious woman whose nickname was "Mommy Dot." Besides being the owner and operator of this camp, she was actively involved with the National Audubon Society. We volunteers were each given specific activity assignments for the summer's sessions. Every two weeks, a new group of disabled children would enroll in the camp. I was asked to be the organizer for special group activities. This was a valuable experience for me. Reflecting back, this was another experience to add to my environmental collections!

After the summer camp, I immediately traveled to South Bend, Indiana, to begin searching for housing quarters. Hadn't had much experience with apartment shopping before. I couldn't afford a very expensive place to rent, so as I scanned the South Bend Tribune paper, I focused upon and rented an apartment at a reasonable fee. Well, this turned out to be a mistake! That first night, I was fraught with what felt like something biting me all night long. I discovered the answer the next morning. I found multiple red skin eruptions scattered over my body, and sure enough, I saw my very first *cimex lectularius* (bedbug). I doubt whether this environmental experience contributed much to my decision-making toward a medical career, at least not at the time. I left those premises and continued looking for a better place to stay. I saw another ad in the rental section of the newspaper. It was from an elderly lady who lived alone, wanting to share her home with a renter. Her name was Mrs. Kaley, who lived on Haley Street. Although I would not have a private entry, the upstairs, including a private bath would be my living quarters; it also included my meals—and best of all, it was free from bedbugs. It didn't take long to come to a verbal contractual agreement. Not only was this to become a very special arrangement for housing, it was located only two blocks from Studebaker School, where I was to be employed. And lastly, Mrs. Kaley claimed me as her "adopted son."

I enjoyed my three years of teaching at Studebaker School. I was well received by the principal, the teachers, and the children I taught. Back in that day, teachers were still very well respected. It was considered honorable to begin each day of school with the Pledge of Allegiance and a prayer, a routine that almost always set the tone for the day. It didn't take long for me to become adjusted to the new school environment and the community as well. Parents would invite me into their homes for an evening meal from time to time. This allowed me to develop a better rapport with the children and the immediate community. Discipline issues were not a great problem. One time, two boys were having an ongoing conflict with each other. I met with them alone outside the classroom to get a better insight of their conflict. After listening to each of their stories, I gave them a week's assignment. It included having each boy writing on paper, every nice thing he observed about the other. At the end of the week, they met with me to report their findings. The one boy said, "He's really a pretty good person." Sometimes girls required a bit of assistance as well. One cute little girl named Martha was frequently disturbing the boys, especially those sitting near her in the back of the classroom. It seemed to be a habitual problem. I got tired of witnessing the ongoing problem, so I had her move her desk belongings to one located in front of my desk. This way I could keep a better eye on her. I noticed Martha spent an excessive amount of time staring at me, so I said to her, "Martha, will you stop disturbing the boys and get to work!" Martha replied, "It's not the boys, Mr. Graber, It's you!" Well, what does one do with that one! *Everybody* burst out laughing! When there was conflict in the classroom that could not be handled by me, full support was available from the school principal.

I could not have asked for anything better in that time frame of my life. I thoroughly enjoyed my time spent teaching school in the elementary grades of South Bend City Schools, especially at the Studebaker Elementary school. It provided me an outstanding environmental experience; I was invited there at the right time and at the right place. I was truly learning to become a real teacher! I had no reason at that time to "peep across the fence for other green pastures," for I was happy with the teaching profession. Yet I could not dismiss the thought of pursuing medicine as my professional calling. I counseled with several highly respected professionals whom I trusted very much but found no answers. Then, one gentleman said to me, "It's very helpful to seek help from trusted individuals, but you are the one who will ultimately need to make that final decision." Looking back, this turned out to be the advice I needed that enabled me to make the right decision for my life's work. But I needed to satisfy one important issue. I had a mediocre freshman year of college, and I did not have an adequate background in mathematics or science in high school; therefore, remedial educational courses needed to be addressed first. I taught one more year at Studebaker Elementary School while I enrolled in night school attending adult high school and college education courses from Indiana University Extension; two being general chemistry and speed reading, plus a college course of algebra. The general chemistry was exceptionally easy. My speed reading increased from three hundred to eight hundred words per minute with associated improvement in comprehension. The college algebra course required more effort (didn't have high school algebra), but I did quite well. Later, I enrolled in a college physics course. Again, I did quite well but realized if I had had a background in geometry, it would have made it even more exciting. After completing college physics, I enrolled in college trigonometry; that was very interesting and easy. All these preliminary scholastic exercises provided me with the confidence I needed to finalize my decision. By this time, I knew within my heart and mind that the time had come to either pursue the path of medicine or lay the idea to rest forever.

Meanwhile, I had been seriously dating a lady school teacher who was a graduate from Goshen College and who was teaching high school home economics and physical education. Her name was Roberta M. Schertz, a brilliant and caring individual. Before college, she had work experience as a bookkeeper in her hometown high school. We discussed my intent to pursue medicine as a career. Her response was forthright, stating, "If that is what God wants you to do, I would support and encourage you to do so." That discussion was very helpful. Being completely supportive, we committed our life to each other and were married on December 22, 1957. Soon after, I submitted my resignation from the City Schools of South Bend, Indiana. Details of that event and the return to college to complete my premedical education courses can be found in the following chapter.

College Graduation photo of Harry Graber 1954

CHAPTER 4

Accepting My Call to Pursue Medicine

The making of a physician is suggestive that the creation
of the physician is in the hands of The Artist; one, who after
multiple attempts of molding, shaping and reshaping,
visualizes his final polished product to be very good.

Back to School to Complete Premedical Courses

I submitted my resignation to the school superintendent of School
City of South Bend, Indiana, at the close of my third year of teaching
in that school system and reentered Goshen College for my premedical
requirements. The resignation from the South Bend School System (SBSS)
apparently did not sit well with the school superintendent. Unknown to
me at that time, a call had been made to the dean of students at Goshen
College, stating that if I would consider returning to the SBSS system,
they would forgive me and keep me on their teaching staff. Little did
the school superintendent and the Goshen College dean know that my
decision to make the change had been carefully thought through, and
this was the direction I had felt God was leading me. As for my school
principal, although she wished I could stay, she supported my decision and
wished me well. She handed me a copy of the letter of recommendation she
had sent to St. Louis University. In it, she stated I was given the highest
performance rating she had given to a teacher since being a principal over
the past twenty-five years. Reflecting back, I consider that an important
recommendation.

After learning about the communication that was going back and forth between the two institutions, I asked to speak to the president of Goshen College. The college president reminded me of my academic records during my first year and a half while attending the institution. He stated I would need to make some A's in my remaining subjects to stand a chance for entry into any medical school. Following that meeting, I was assigned to H. Clair Amstutz, MD, to be my counselor. During the first semester of that school year, I enrolled in general biology, comparative anatomy, general chemistry, organic chemistry, and qualitative analysis. This was a bit more than I thought I could handle at that given time, so after the first three weeks of school, I dropped the course in qualitative analysis. The second semester was the same as the first, except I enrolled in embryology in the place of comparative anatomy (the latter being a one semester course). This was a big assignment, but I completed the year quite successfully. Before the end of the first semester of classes, a physician friend talked me into taking the AMCAT (aptitude test). I thought the idea was a little premature because I had wanted to complete all my required courses before taking that test.

The AMCAT test was held at Notre Dame University in late autumn. It was a timed test, but I completed it on schedule. After taking the examination, my thoughts were, *Well, I guess that takes care of me.* Meanwhile, the same physician friend once again talked me into applying to several medical schools. It was already January 1960. This was quite late in the year to make application to any medical school and expect to be accepted into the fall term. In fact, St. Louis University School of Medicine was the only school that accepted applications through January. In the meantime, I enrolled in my last required subject, quantitative analysis, at the University of Notre Dame. While attending school there, I received two positive answers. One, I learned I must have done well on my AMCAT (back then, no one found out the results of their scores). Two, St. Louis University must have been satisfied enough to have invited me for an interview during Easter vacation (during the early 1960s, medical schools became interested in accepting students with professional backgrounds apart from the sciences). This gave me additional hope. It was in August 1960 when I received the exciting news. I was accepted to begin my freshman year of medical school at St. Louis University School of Medicine.

We didn't waste much time in making a fast trip to St. Louis, Missouri, to visit the medical center and to search for an apartment. During the same trip, my wife made arrangements to see the superintendent of the St. Louis Public Schools to obtain an application to teach in the city system. Everything worked out quite well. We found a nice air-conditioned apartment, and my wife was hired to teach physical education at the junior high school level.

Up to this time, the reader has been privileged to learn about some key environmental experiences of mine. Had it not been for the insight and Godly wisdom of my mother and favorite college professor, Dr. Mary Royer, there would be no need to continue on with my story. As it is, we will now get into the nitty-gritty on *The Making of a Physician*.

The Making of a Physician Is a Continuum

As stated above, the *making of a physician* suggests that the formation of the physician is in the hands of our Creator, who, after multiple attempts of molding, shaping, and reshaping our lives, visualizes His final polished product to be good. That molding and reshaping becomes a lifelong adventurous process; it represents a continuum.

As I look back upon my road less traveled, it still appears as an indelible dream to me, that it occurred just yesterday. I can still sense the nervousness intertwined with excitement and emotion. It is for these reasons I am still able to present a vivid accounting of most of the adventurous happenings that occurred to me, during my four years of medical school: learning the basic language and fundamentals of medicine at St. Louis University School of Medicine.

Time moved swiftly. It was September 1960, and I was one of 119 other first-year medical students officially known as the freshman class. As was the standard, all medical students were appropriately suited in white, short-length coats, shirt, and black tie. It was exciting, but I was somewhat frightened what the days ahead would bring to me. I would soon find out.

Little did I know what to expect from one professor to another. Some professors were outstanding researchers but appeared to have limited teaching skills. Others, because of their native language, made it difficult for one to understand. Fortunately, there was a third category: those who were experienced teachers. They all had one thing in common. They all lectured faster than one could keep up with notetaking. So I had to make an early adjustment: take notes with greater speed! Most of the lecturers covered about fifty pages or more of material per session. Imagine attending three to four separate class settings like this in a given day. Notetaking was almost impossible, at least at first. I learned I had to write one to two legible letters in a given word, the rest being a straight line in between. At the end of each day, I would go back over my notes and fill in the missing letters of each important word. No wonder physicians have such horrible cursive writing habits! Another early thing I learned: do not misinterpret a professor's instructions. For example, the professor of gross anatomy, who was an outstanding lecturer, had a different perception of the word "slow" than did some of his students. Before handing out the first major written test to our class, it was clearly stated that we could take our time answering each question. As I began looking at the questions, I found them to be very reasonable and easy to answer, but I took my time with each one as I thought we were privileged to do. After completing seventy of the one hundred questions on the test, the professor said, "Time is up. Hand in your test papers." I couldn't believe he said that! We were told we may take our time answering the questions. The next day, the professor stated in a friendly manner, "For those of you who didn't do too well on the test, feel free to come in to see me." So I decided to go in to see the professor. I wanted to mention that I had understood him say we could take our time with the test. After I had explained my reason for not being able to complete the test, he said, "If you can't work faster than that, you don't belong here." Several lessons were learned from that early encounter: (1) "Take your time" has a relative meaning, so thereafter, I increased my speed. (2) There is a catch to "Feel free to come in to see me." I quickly learned that he is the professor, and I am the student. I never had to be reminded about my lack of speed, again. An upperclassman, who was also my friend, said to me, "Just run scared!" That early incident was troubling to me. It took several months for me to adjust and shake off an attitude of mistrust when taking a written examination. But eventually, I accepted and understood that these early experiences were for my good in helping me to become a true physician.

A second early medical school adjustment was to see and personally handle a variety of chemically preserved human organ specimens, each with a different pathological disease entity. Seeing these specimens for the first time required a brief period of time in getting used to. First was the appearance. Second was the adjustment to the odor of formaldehyde, which also caused burning of the eyes. To see and handle these specimens was extremely important for our learning, especially in the courses of histology, pathology, and gross anatomy. In gross anatomy class, we learned how to properly dissect and identify all parts of the human body. At the beginning of our lab experience, it was made very clear that all students must handle the cadavers with an attitude of sacredness and respect for the human body. This was a mandatory principle. These privileged educational experiences were a part of our early learning requirements and were essential toward *the making of a physician*. The next paragraph is intended to help the reader gain further insight regarding the intensity and depth of learning required of every student during the first and second year, before moving on to the next level. Near the end of the second year, the student will be taught how to perform a proper physical examination on healthy patients (on each other).

Seeing, handling, and identifying all the anatomical body parts in anatomy class were a necessity and a prerequisite to achieve an in-depth understanding how the different organ systems functioned in a coordinated manner for the good of the entire body. The second year courses included human physiology, pathology, microbiology, infectious diseases, biochemistry, and pharmacology to name a few. In pharmacology, we needed to not only learn the basic chemistry of the different classes of drugs but also learn what, where, and how they worked, including how they were metabolized (broken down) in the human body. This was a comprehensive year for learning. What has been shared was to provide a superficial idea of what medical school environment is like. Although it was extremely exciting, I never experienced such intensity for detailed learning in my life. There was no time for play. After the completion of the second year of school, the student should have acquired an in-depth understanding of how the body functions in the healthy state. What I have shared does not provide justice to all the subjects to which we were introduced. Neither does it do justice to what all the students were required to learn, but it should shed some light into the magnitude of subject matter that was expected for every medical student to learn in a very limited period of time. Before introducing the educational experiences of student's clinical training (that is, learning to care for patients with their illnesses, under the supervision of professional physicians), the reader should know that formal didactic classes were held along with the "hands on" training experiences. This included courses in general medicine, psychiatry, and general surgery, plus all the other subspecialties.

Near the end of the second year of medical school, we students were introduced to "how to perform a proper physical examination" on normal subjects (students). This was exciting! Eli Lilly provided each student a stethoscope, a tuning fork, a percussion hammer, and medical bag (still have my original). By this time, our brains were "figuratively swollen" from all that knowledge we had accumulated, but with zero experience. Fortunately, back in the 1960s, a major emphasis was placed upon performing a proper physical examination. Unfortunately, expertise did not occur in a six-week learning course, but it was a start. Having been exposed to excellent teachers of "basic medical education," we were well on our way to be introduced and trained for the clinical years of medicine. Our subjects were live persons, many of whom were victims of a variety of diseases. Our first assignments included learning to obtain a thorough history and perform a proper physical examination and present it to a faculty physician—might suggest it's best when one has all the data complete and correct. There was no time limit to workdays. The end of the day was when all assignments were completed. In addition to the required daytime duties, we were also responsible to continue with our studies from textbooks, as before—training days for future years! It was hard work and long hours, but with results that paid off. It's interesting how much didactic material one can remember fifty-plus years ago, even though one has never encountered the clinical problem—such as developing *vitamin A toxicity* from eating polar bear liver or developing *vitamin B12 deficiency* from eating a fish in Alaskan waters infested with a certain tapeworm (*Diphyllobothrium*). A little humor mixed in with a didactic subject shouldn't hurt anybody; might even wake one up.

Before bringing closure to this educational topic, I would like to share several stories. In our clinical years of training, there were certain experiences which are retained as fresh memories—some of extreme importance, and others of a humorous nature. Two of these come to mind. The first was an incident that included the chief of cardiovascular surgery, his chief resident, and myself (senior medical student). It was an era when heart surgery was still in its infancy. A patient was scheduled for a "closed mitral commissurotomy" (a surgical procedure to open up the leaflets of the mitral valve in selective patients with mitral stenosis). (Reference: *Annals of Surgery* by Dr. C. R. Hanlon, et al., St. Louis University, 1968). The chief surgical resident was assigned to assist the chief of surgery with this procedure. He apparently had some conflict, so he asked me to "scrub in" to assist the surgeon. Now, I was only a senior medical student, but apparently I was thought to be "skillfully trustworthy" by the surgical resident's standard. I didn't know what to say! If I said no, I would be in trouble, and the same would be true if I said yes. Well, I scrubbed in to assist; put on a sterile gown, cap, booties, and mask; and walked into the surgical suit to be first assistant for the surgery. The cardiovascular surgeon glanced at me but didn't say a word. I remained silent too. I followed his commands the best I could. Fortunately, everything went smoothly. I don't know what transpired in follow-up between the chief resident and his superior, but I bet it wasn't pretty. What made this such an unusual incident was medical students were never allowed to be on the same hospital floor when the chief, vice chief, and the third surgeon in line were making teaching rounds with their surgical residents. The second story relates to two lectures that were given to us senior medical students on the topic of *caring for the dying patient*. The professor who was lecturing said, "When caring for a dying patient, the physician is responsible to share two important matters: one, ask the patient if he/she has taken care of all their earthly responsibilities and two, ask the patient if they made final plans for their Heavenly Home." I was much impressed with those two lectures—to hear this from a physician of his stature made a lasting impression on me.

I remain highly privileged to have attended a Judeo-Christian medical school such as St. Louis University. It was a perfect fit. It helped to strengthen my own spiritual values in life and provided me with the proper training in caring for my future patients.

St. Louis University Medical School Graduates of 1964

The final celebration for the 1964 graduating class of St. Louis University medical students was at hand. One hundred four of the original one hundred twenty freshman medical students were eagerly waiting to receive their coveted diplomas. Much hard work and many long hours of in-depth study finally paid off. The class of 1964 sat near the front of the auditorium in alphabetical order, each wearing a black gown with a green *hood*, representing the medical profession. On stage sat the prestigious medical faculty, beginning with the president, vice president, dean, associate dean, assistant deans, and the chairman faculty members of each of their different departments. Then, there were the people sitting in the auditorium, including family members and other interested persons, some of whom traveled great distances to honor this graduating class of 1964. My wife and my parents were among them, with satisfied expressions on their faces, waiting for the ceremony to begin. I wonder what my mother was thinking. After the presentations of honors and awards were given to selective class members, the time came for the graduating class to recite the Hippocratic Oath as arranged by St. Louis Guild of the Catholic Medical Association. It reads as follows:

> I swear in the presence of the Almighty and before my family, my teachers and my peers that according to my ability and judgement I will keep this oath and stipulation.
>
> To reckon all who have taught me this art equally dear to me as my parents and in this same spirit and dedication to impart knowledge of the art of medicine. I will treat without exception all who seek my ministrations, so long as the treatment of others is not compromised thereby, and I will seek the counsel

of particularly skilled physicians where indicated for the benefit of my patient.

I will follow that method of treatment which according to my ability and judgement, I consider for the benefit of my patient and abstain from what ever is harmful or mischievous. I will neither prescribe nor administer a lethal dose of medicine to any patient even if asked nor counsel any such thing nor perform act or omission with direct intent deliberately to end a human life. I will maintain the utmost respect for every human life from fertilization to natural death and reject abortion that deliberately takes a human life from fertilization to natural death and reject abortion that deliberately takes a human life.

With purity, holiness and beneficence I will pass my life and practice my art. Except for the prudent correction of an imminent danger, I will neither treat any patient nor carry out any research on any human being without the valid informed consent of the subject or the appropriate legal protector thereof, understanding that research must have as its purpose the furtherance of the health of the individual. Into whatever patient setting I enter, I will go for the benefit of the sick and will abstain from voluntary act of mischief or corruption and further from the seduction of any patient. Whatever in connection with my professional practice or not in connection with it, I may see or hear in the lives of my patients which ought not be spoken abroad, I will not divulge, reckoning that all such should be kept secret.

While I continue to keep this Oath non-violated, may it be granted to me to enjoy life and the practice of the art and science of medicine with the blessing of the Almighty and respected by my peers and society, but should I tresspass and violate this oath, may the reverse be my lot.

Following the recitation of the oath, the Class of 1964 lined up in alphabetical order to receive our well-deserved diplomas. Needless to say, this was an early highlight of our lives. We were now recognized as physicians. However, little did we realize that we were still "a little green around the gills."

Photo of Dr. Harry L. Graber
(graduation picture from St. Louis U. School of Medicine, 1964

CHAPTER 5

Postgraduate Medical Training Follows Medical School

There will be times in life that special events happen
for a given purpose, only to be understood as *providential,*
years later. This forthcoming story was one of those.

All medical school graduates are required to successfully pass a written examination from within the state they had trained before entering into the practice of medicine. Many states will accept the results of the exam that was successfully completed by reciprocity. Example: graduating from a medical school in the state of Missouri, I became licensed in that state, but also in the state of Ohio, by reciprocity. Although one could have practiced general medicine after successfully passing the state board exam in certain states (in 1964), this was highly fraught against. However, it was then not uncommon after graduating from a medical school to begin practicing general medicine after the completion of one year of *internship* training.

Following graduation from St. Louis University School of Medicine, I applied and was accepted to begin my postgraduate training at the Akron General Hospital in Akron, Ohio. My goal was to either enter into *family medicine* or *internal medicine.* After the completion of my internship training, I spent my second year in the family medicine program—I wanted additional pediatric medicine training. Near the close of my second year of postgraduate education, I was ready to further my training in internal medicine, which meant two additional years of residency. The postgraduate program at Akron General Hospital was perfect for me. It was academic yet clinically oriented. I became a very zealous and committed student and received the *Intern of the Year Award* for those efforts. Near the end of my second year of postgraduate education, I received an interesting *"call in the night"*! That call brought about an interruption of my original plans but later proved to be an asset to the completion of my residency training in internal medicine.

A Call in the Night

"Hello! Is this Dr. Graber?" I answered, "Yes, this is Dr. Graber. May I ask to whom am I speaking?" "This is Dr. Paul Hooley, from DeGraff, Ohio." I looked at my watch. It was eleven o'clock at night—the voice sounded so tired! He was still seeing patients in his rural office at eleven o'clock at night—I could hardly believe it. As the conversation went on, I learned Dr. Hooley was wanting to get acquainted with me and inviting me to set up practice of medicine in DeGraff, Ohio. I had never been to DeGraff, nor did I know where it was located. I hardly knew what to answer, so I told him I needed some time to think about it. I had mixed feelings. I was in the middle of my medical residency training, and I wasn't really thinking about settling in a rural area. Besides, this was the second request I had received to set up my medical practice. The other was from a very close teacher friend who had been wooing me to return to South Bend, Indiana, to work there. I thanked Dr. Hooley and promised I would return his call after I had time to consider his offer.

After a couple of weeks, I returned the call and made arrangements to meet with Dr. Hooley and several other men to learn more about what he had in mind. As it turned out, the proposal was for me to settle in the village of DeGraff and set up my office practice of medicine there. He went on to say he was planning to construct a new medical building near West Liberty, Ohio, which would be designed for two physicians. A physician was already committed to join him at the new site. I listened to the plan but said I was not interested. He and those with him didn't know what to say. Then one gentlemen suggested maybe the West Liberty community could handle a third person instead of two. This sounded more attractive, so I said I would come for one year, then return to Akron to complete my residency training. After that, I would return as a specialist in internal medicine. That seemed to satisfy everyone concerned. There was no written contract but a gentleman's handshake. This was in 1965. I kept my promise and dropped out of my training for one year to join Drs. Paul Hooley and Glen Miller at what became known as Oak Hill

Medical Associates, located on U.S. 68, about three miles north of West Liberty, Ohio. When the time came, my wife and I, along with our three little children, settled in a rented house in the village of West Liberty, Ohio. One of my first stops was to visit the local People's Savings and Loan to ask for a short-term loan, for I was nearly out of money. I asked Mr. Hook, the president, if I could borrow $100 to carry me through the next couple of weeks. I informed him that my family and I had just moved into the community and was recently employed as a physician by Oak Hill Medical Associates of West Liberty. The gentleman smiled and granted me a $200 loan.

As an introduction to the new Logan County community, I was asked to be on family medicine call the very first weekend of my arrival. This meant that I would be responsible for any medical problems arising from the Oak Hill Medical patients, as well as being on emergency call for the Mary Rutan Hospital emergency room. For me, being new and inexperienced, it felt somewhat monumental. Fortunately, the only call I received was to care for a gentleman who had lacerated one of his fingers and required some suturing.

The following Monday was my first official day of work. I vividly remember that day. I felt somewhat slighted. Only three patients came to see me. But it didn't take long for business to improve. Probably some of the earlier patients came to me just to meet the newest "kid on the block." Routine office charges were $3 per visit, which meant I contributed $9 to the coffer my first day. My monthly salary for that first year was $800. It proved to be a valuable and adventurous beginning, filled with many educational experiences. By the way, I earned enough money to pay off my $200 loan and provide care for my young family.

As agreed, after spending one year with Oak Hill Medical Associates, I returned to the Akron Medical Center to complete my residency training. It had been an exciting year and extremely helpful for the clinical experience I received. It provided me with excellent insight and gave me a better grasp upon what I should be focusing upon during the remainder of my training years. Looking back, I could not have asked for a better way to complete my formal medical residency training. These environmental adventures provided another unique milestone toward the making of a physician.

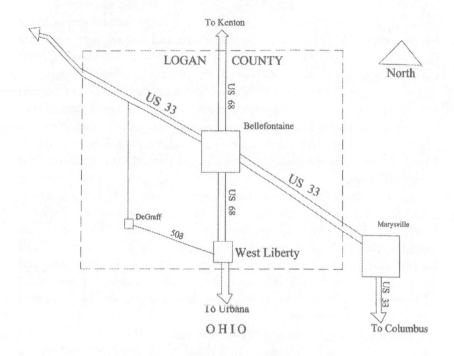

Map of Logan County, Ohio
(DeGraff, West Liberty, Bellefontaine, Ohio)

Back to Complete My Internal Medicine Residency Training

It was July 1967 when my wife and I, along with our three little children, started back to Akron, Ohio, to complete my medical residency training. We were fortunate to rent a house that had been very recently vacated in Cuyahoga Falls, Ohio (almost a twin city with Akron) by a pediatric medical resident who had just completed his training. Looking back at those early years, I find it hard to realize the patience and willingness that Roberta was willing to endure. This represented the seventh year of our vagabond lifestyle. And though she may have shed silent tears, I don't recall that happening. Her commitment to this "calling" at times seemed stronger than my own.

I had two more years of medical residency training to complete until becoming an official board-qualified medical internist. I was eager to begin! Most of this training took place within the hospital setting. However, some of the instructors invited me to go with them to their private offices as well. These were two important years to glean maximum intellect and hands-on experience from patients under the umbrella of my multiple subspecialty instructors. During these two years, I was able to develop procedural skills with good technique and gain expertise in caring for patients. In my last year of training, I was assigned to become chief resident of medicine, which meant I would be held accountable for some of the teaching to certain medical residents under me. It also meant I would be in charge of providing total care of the patients who had no private physician. In this setting, a staff physician would accompany me to assist in the care of these patients. The instructors were very eager to share their knowledge and expertise with any of us, as long as we showed interest. My interest was intense. I spent many after-work hours at the hospital with different physician instructors, digesting as much knowledge as I could. There was very little free time. The free time that I had, I spent reading from my *Cecil and Loeb Textbook of Medicine*. Not only did I underline most of the textbook, but I also wrote a formal outline and made tapes of all my outline notes. Not one time did I waver from my commitment.

Additional Assignments

During my residency, we who were in training were given special assignments to present formal conferences for the faculty and all other physicians in training. Some of these were assigned topics, and others could be approved topics of our choosing. One required educational exercise before graduation included an assigned case study of a patient whose disease entity was unknown to the presenter. It was the responsibility of the assigned resident physician to review the case carefully, including all tests that were done; review the medical literature; and then come up with what was felt to be an appropriate differential diagnoses. From the differential diagnosis, the assignee was asked to propose the correct diagnosis and give valid reasoning for making that decision. To do this intellectual exercise properly, one had to do a lot of reading to prove that the diagnosis was correct. Not only did this include giving a proposed correct diagnosis, but it also provided appropriate reasoning that led one to that conclusion. This was exciting and fun as I look back upon those training days, but at times, there were some nervous moments indeed. I recall at one given conference I was asked a specific question. Apparently, I gave a "roundabout" answer, and the physician instructor said, "Cut out the B.S., Graber." Lesson to be learned was, if one is not sure or absolutely does not know, it's best to say, "I don't know." And this can also get one into trouble. One other time I had stated that I did not know the answer to a certain question, and the professor said, "I want you to have the answer before the sun goes down." To this day, I don't know which was the best solution, but I do know somehow it brings about humility and, hopefully, maturity.

Research Participation

Besides being involved with the formal programmed activities of my medical residency training, I was invited to participate in a very interesting clinical research study. It was a time in U.S. history, including the Akron community, when there was a noticeable increase of nonsterile abortions being performed, mostly among poor young women, during their first trimester of pregnancy. Many of these individuals were already in advanced stages of septic shock when they arrived at the hospital emergency room. Most of them died. Clinical researchers across the country had spent many hours searching for better ways to care for these patients. Dr. J. L. Berk, et al.,* of Case Western Reserve University of Cleveland, Ohio, represented one of the many groups attempting to tackle this problem. His research work was first carried out in the laboratory, using canines as subjects that were in early septic shock (shock resulting from bacteria in the bloodstream), treating them with intravenous *propanolol* (a beta-blocking agent). It had already been known that individuals in septic shock presented in high-output congestive heart failure, secondary to the formation of AV shunting of blood, affecting different organs. It was postulated that propanolol corrected the problem of shunting in these organs. The next phase of his clinical research was to use the drug in humans who presented to the hospital with sepsis. My assignment, when called in to help care for these septic shock patients, was to assist in measuring their cardiac output. The measurement of cardiac output helped to provide proper volume of intravenous fluid replacement. Those interested with this study may refer to Berk, J. L.; Hagen, J. F.; Dunn, J. M. The role of beta adrenergic blockade in the treatment of septic shock. *Surgical Gynecological Obstetrics,* 1970, 130:1025–34.*

After Medical Residency Came Medical Boards

The American Board on Medical Specialties (AMBS) was introduced in 1933. Today, approximately 80 percent of specialty-trained physicians are boarded. Headquarters is in Chicago, Illinois. Physicians who have successfully completed their specialty requirements are known to be specialty eligible. Those who have successfully passed the specialty examination are known to be specialty boarded.

After the completion of my three-year medical residency training, I became a *qualified internal medical specialist*. My eventual goal was to also become *board certified*. Back in the mid-1960s, at least at the center where I had trained, the first-attempt "passing rate" was 35 percent. Although a monumental goal, I was determined I was not going to become a part of those statistics. That was a highly regarded motivating force that helped me to give my best effort on the first attempt. From childhood on up, I had been known to be a very competitive athlete. That is why I highly regard sports to be an important part of one's environmental experiences. During those early years, internal medicine boards included two parts. *Part I* was a written examination, and *Part II* was an oral examination. The second part was offered one year after successfully passing the written exam and included a favorable letter of reference sent by a certified *internal medicine specialist*.

While a number of my medical colleagues spent an excess amount of their "free time" playing pool, etc., my efforts were directed toward serious studying. I was determined I would not take the exam more than once. Although I did not claim to be the brightest student, I felt well prepared for that written examination. The effort paid off. That special letter was delivered to me after I had already returned to Bellefontaine, Ohio. The medical nurse at the office handed the envelope to me. There was no way I was going to open that letter in front of everybody, so I excluded myself to go to the office and close the door. With some tremor, I opened the envelope, and to my delight, it stated *"Congratulations on successfully passing the written examination!"* That was a very happy day in my early medical life as a physician. I shared the letter to the rest of the medical office staff members.

One year later, I received a letter by invitation, to take my Part II, Internal Medicine Oral Examination, at the University of Minnesota. The content of the letter stated that I would be required to obtain a history and perform a thorough physical examination on two patients, allowing one hour per patient. My medical examiner would be Richard V. Ebert, MD, chairman of the American Board of Internal Medicine. Just reading those instructions was enough to introduce a little nervousness. Remember, I had already returned back to work for a little more than one year. Besides being very busy in my new practice of internal medicine, I continued to put every extra effort I had, in preparation for the Part II examination. As was the case with the Part I board exam, I felt well prepared.

I boarded a plane the night before the examination. En route to Minneapolis, Minnesota, the plane had stopped at an airport. Remember, it was nighttime, and I was excited. I thought the plane had landed at the Minneapolis International Airport, so I got off the plane to get a shuttle bus to my hotel. As luck would have it, it was not where I was to get off. I ran as fast as I could go, carrying my "carry-on case." Fortunately, I made it back onto the plane just before takeoff, heading for the Minneapolis Airport.

The night was short, and I did not sleep very well. I flagged a taxicab to take me to the university medical center. I arrived in good time and waited to meet the medical resident, who was to introduce me to the patients I was to evaluate. Unfortunately, the medical resident physician had overslept, so instead of allowing me one hour per patient, I was given only forty-five minutes to evaluate each one (my examiner was not informed of the medical resident's blunder). *What a bummer!* Needless to say, not only did I feel cheated, but I also found it difficult to keep my poise. The first patient presented with pulmonic stenosis (partial obstruction of the pulmonic valve). The second patient was an alcoholic by history with the typical findings of early jaundice, enlarged spleen, mild ascites (small collection of fluid within the abdominal space), and telangiectasia (shunting of blood of small blood vessels beneath the skin) just above the nail beds of his fingers. Having to rush through the examination, I missed finding the enlarged spleen. When Dr. Ebert asked me what abnormalities I found on the second patient, I did not mention the enlargement of the spleen. He then proceeded to put up the radio isotope film on the lighted screen and asked, "What do you think?" I replied, "I think I missed the enlarged spleen." He then asked me several questions about jaundice (involving Bilirubin— direct and indirect), which was very easy to answer. Lastly, we went to the patient, and he asked me to explain the small red spots on the patient's skin, just above the nail beds of the fingers. I explained the telangiectasia on the dorsum (top) of the fingers and provided him with a reference that supported my explanation. He had no further questions, and he said I was finished with the examination.

I was relieved that the oral medical board examination was over. I must admit, I had some early doubts about my results. I was considering writing Dr. Ebert a letter explaining to him about the "sleep in" problem with the chief medical resident, but my better judgment told me to postpone that letter for the time being. Two weeks later, I received that important letter from Dr. Ebert. I was hesitant to open it. As I did so, my heart was pounding with fear of what I would see. The first word I read was "Congratulations!" I had successfully passed my oral examination, and I was now considered a certified internal medicine specialist. Looking back at that moment of my life, I am grateful I had admitted to Dr. Ebert that I had missed the physical finding of an enlarged spleen on that patient. Having made an excuse for that error could have cost me my certification.

Beginning My Long-Term Commitment at Mary Rutan Hospital and Oak Hill Medical Associates

My role as the first board-certified internist of Logan County, Ohio, began in 1969. Awaiting me was the assignment to become the first director of a newly established *intensive care unit*, carefully envisioned and planned by Dr. Paul Hooley, et al. Though smaller, this was a state-of- the-art unit comparable to others that were erected at larger medical centers. It wasn't long after my arrival that I became exceedingly busy. Almost more than I could handle! I found myself caring for approximately thirty-five in-house patients per day, including my days off. Some of the patients' illnesses were quite difficult to manage. I was greatly in need of help. Fortunately, my colleague, Dr. Glen Miller, sensed my need and took a sabbatical leave to become trained and certified in internal medicine (1971–1973), but that was still two years away.

Case Presentations

To provide some idea of the volume and complexity of the patients' illnesses I cared for, I am including summaries of six patients. Three of the patients were treated in the new ICCU facility. A fourth patient who was hospitalized for a medical workup was cared for in a regular room. The fifth case was an emergency request by the director of nursing, who described a patient developing progressive symptoms of dyspnea (shortness of breath), associated with an increased heart rate and the finding of moist rales (fluid) in the bases of both lungs. The sixth patient presented in the emergency room with no obtainable blood pressure.

Case no. 1. This was a young teenager who had aborted a fetus and developed septicemia. She had already been receiving intravenous antibiotics. She was in shock and renal shutdown. I was consulted to manage the patient. It is of interest in that I had been a part of a research team while in training at the Akron General Medical Center, caring for such patients that I am describing here. I made a decision to use intravenous propranolol, the same drug we used at the medical center while in training.

This was a difficult decision to make, because in the *Hippocratic Oath,* as arranged by the St. Louis Guild of the Catholic Medical Association, it stated, "Except for the prudent correction of an imminent danger, I will neither treat any patient nor carry out any research on any human being without the valid informed consent of the subject." We discussed this issue and followed the proper protocol before infusing the medication intravenously. Within twenty-four hours, the young lady was awake and her kidneys began to function. Soon after, the patient was back to normal and was dismissed from the hospital. I had the privilege to see this young lady sometime later. This was more than a coincidence to have had previous experience with Propranolol and fluid replacement in the treatment of septic shock during my medical residency training.

Case no. 2. One night, a grandmother and her granddaughter presented to our hospital emergency room. The young girl was already unconscious. Both were victims of carbon monoxide inhalation from a faulty chimney. This was a very difficult problem to treat. The red blood cells (RBCs) normally transport oxygen to all cells of the body. Because carbon monoxide, when inhaled, has a greater affinity for the RBCs, it displaces the oxygen molecule from the RBCs. If not corrected, the patient will soon die. The best treatment I could provide, back in those years, was to deliver 100 percent oxygen with an oxygen mask to the two patients. It wasn't long before grandmother was alert. I stayed at the bedside of the young girl all night. By morning, she began to regain consciousness. Within two days, she was ready to be discharged from the hospital. Years later, I had the privilege to attend the granddaughter's wedding. At my first retirement, the grandmother presented me with a special doll to remind me of her granddaughter on that dreadful night and the life-saving treatment they had received.

Case no. 3. A young lady in her early twenties was referred to me to evaluate a problem of intermittent hypertension, associated with nighttime sweating, and cervical lymph nodes of the neck. Because of these symptoms, I admitted the patient to the hospital to evaluate her for a possible tumor-secreting hormone, called *pheochromocytoma.* The workup included collecting twenty-four urine specimens and several blood tests to evaluate for excess epinephrine and norepinephrine (adrenaline and noradrenaline) levels. While attending to other hospitalized patients, I received an emergency call to this patient's room. Upon arrival, the young lady was fighting for her last breath. Her lungs had already filled up with fluid. She was in acute pulmonary edema (acute heart failure). Before anything could be done, the patient died. This was a very sad, sudden, and unexpected death. The autopsy showed a large *pheochromocytoma* tumor located in the area of *Zucherkandl* (where the common iliac arteries branch off from the lower abdominal aorta). The blood and urine studies showed elevations of epinephrine and norepinephrine, positive for the secreting tumor. Although nothing could be done in 1969 to save this young lady, there might have been an opportunity if this had occurred several years later and at a large medical center. *Pheochromocytoma* tumors are rare. Although most of them are located within the midportion of the adrenal glands, some, like this one, are located outside of those glands and are considered malignant. Unfortunately, an experience such as this also becomes incorporated into the making of a physician, memories of which never fade away.

Case no. 4. One day, when attending to my patients in the hospital, I received a call to quickly go to a patient's room who was developing progressive shortness of breath. This was not one of my assigned patients to take care of. I quickly reviewed the lady's medical record and learned she was admitted to the hospital with hyperthyroidism. There were no monitors available to detect what type of an arrhythmia she might be having (our only monitors were in intensive care). A quick physical examination of the patient revealed she was in acute pulmonary edema (acute congestive heart failure with fluid in the bases of the lungs). The heart rate was regular but exceeding one hundred beats per minute. Because of the urgency of the problem, I quickly applied tourniquets to all extremities, releasing one in a rotational manner every five minutes. I gave four milligrams of IV morphine and performed a phlebotomy, removing approximately 150 cc of venous blood. Back in that era of medicine, this was a typical way to manage acute pulmonary edema. An electrocardiogram showed a sinus tachycardia, without any other abnormalities. Within about five minutes, the patient was breathing more comfortably, and the lungs revealed better breath sounds. The tourniquets were kept on the extremities for another fifteen or more minutes, releasing one at a time over the next twenty to thirty minutes. The patient was started on a digitalis and diuretic. Because of the associated problem of hyperthyroidism (a cause for AV shunting), propanolol was also started. After the patient's condition became stable, I called her physician and husband. The primary physician followed through with treating the patient's overactive thyroid and the associated heart failure problem.

Case no. 5. I was asked to see and manage a patient who was transferred into the new ICCU unit with a problem of hypotension, associated with a bacterial infection. Prior to this admission, the patient had been on long-term corticosteriods (cortisone) for the treatment of her arthritis. This part of the patient's history was extremely important, because long-term usage of a corticosteroid depresses the outer part (cortex) of the adrenal gland. Hence, not only is the adrenal gland suppressed in function, but the electrolytes (sodium and potassium) become imbalanced. By providing the patient with a corticosteroid replacement along with a proper antibiotic, the blood pressure became stable. After the patient was free of her infection, the corticosteroid was gradually decreased over a period of time and eventually discontinued. The patient was later dismissed from the intensive care unit and referred back to her primary physician.

Case no. 6. A lady of middle age presented to the hospital emergency room alert but without a blood pressure. She had been stung by a bee (she was known to be allergic to bee stings). An intravenous line was immediately started, and epinephrine was administered per bolus and then by IV drip infusion. Not long after a blood pressure was palpable and later by sphygmomanometry (blood pressure cuff). Within one-half hour, the patient's condition stabilized.

These six cases represent different types of problems that internal medicine specialists may be called upon to consult and assist in the management of patients who are typically referred into modern intensive care units requiring sophisticated technological equipment. We were fortunate to have had the newly constructed ICCU in 1969 (technological equipment in hospitals became available as a result of the exploration of outer space programs). Consider the disadvantages physicians had in caring for their patients without the technology prior to that time. Today, technology has become extremely sophisticated nearly replacing the need for the stethoscope. Therefore, it is absolutely imperative that all physicians make every effort to stay abreast with the important advancements in medicine. I became cognizant of that concern very early in my career, and it became the main driving force for me to take advantage of every opportunity to remain on the cutting edge of medicine. I cannot be more forthright than to keep repeating "The making of a physician is a continuum." It is not a onetime adventurous learning experience. The only time one can feel tempted to say "I have finally arrived" at that milestone is at the time of one's retirement. For if one does slack off, it will breed contentment, and contentment will result in complacency, and complacency will result in poor patient care. More of this latter concern will be addressed in chapter 8 when I discuss "Who is Mary Rutan?"

CHAPTER 6

A Second Long-Distance Call

Actually, this became my fifth call. The first was to dedicate my life to God. The second one, my professor told me she thought God had something else for me, other than becoming a teacher. The third was a calling to become a physician. The fourth was a call to come to Bellefontaine, Ohio—and now, what could this call be?

In 1973, I received a long-distance phone call from Ohio State University. The voice said "Is this Dr. Graber?" I replied, "Yes, this is Dr. Graber." He went on to say, "This is Dr. Charles Wooley from Ohio State University." I remembered him quite well. We were both board members of the Central Ohio Heart Association, and also, I had referred many of my patients with heart disease to him. After a further brief conversation, he asked, "Have you ever considered receiving more formal training in cardiology?" I told him that I had not but would be interested in considering it. I'm not certain why Dr. Wooley should ask me if I had ever considered receiving more training in cardiology, but apparently he felt I needed it. This was very interesting. As the conversation continued, I learned he had already outlined a special program for me at Ohio State University with the Division of Cardiology. But before I go any further with this part of the story, let me reminisce for a moment. Looking back at those years, I wonder if Dr. Wooley was thinking, *What would it be like to formally train someone in cardiology to function in a rural setting, such as Bellefontaine, Ohio?* Indeed, this would be a new concept and probably the first of its kind in a rural setting in the state of Ohio.

It did not take very long to give Dr. Wooley an affirmative answer. What a privilege I was about to have working under him! I shared the invitation with my colleagues, Drs. Paul Hooley and Glen Miller. I asked them for a sabbatical leave to enter into a one-year cardiology fellowship training program at Ohio State University. Approval was granted (Oakhill Medical Associates already had a plan for sabbatical leaves). This did place an increased burden on Dr. Miller, because the two of us were already quite busy.

I began my cardiology training at Ohio State University in July 1974. The cardiology program was specifically structured for the training of a *noninvasive cardiologist* (e.g., excluding heart catheterizations, etc.), designed for a physician working in a rural setting. I would be under Dr. Wooley's tutelage. The curriculum would include clinical research, performing and interpreting echocardiograms, didactic training in nuclear medicine, performing and interpreting stress testing, interpreting electrocardiograms, and participating in a weekly outpatient clinic with Dr. Wooley. This meant that I could learn from a *master cardiologist* how to perform proper cardiovascular examinations on patients presenting with complex heart problems. In addition, I would also be scheduled to rotate through electrophysiology and cardiac catheterization laboratories. Along with three other cardiology fellows, I would be assigned to prepare and present educational topics on a rotational basis (in-depth review of the literature was essential in preparation for these assignments). Other daily conferences included interpretations of electrocardiograms, echocardiograms, and heart catheterization studies. Quizzing the cardiology fellows was the name of the game. Were we nervous? Frequently so, but all the perceived pressure that was placed upon us was for the purpose in making us expert cardiologists. Before discussing my clinical research assignments, I would like to share several unrelated highlights of my time spent while with the Division of Cardiology at Ohio State University.

You see, I was about ten years older than the other cardiology fellows who were in training with me at the University. Because of this age difference, I suspected I was treated a bit differently. Anyway, one day, Dr. Wooley asked me, "Do you have a minute?" I said, "Sure." He invited me to go along with him, but where and for what reason, I did not know. Upon arriving to our destination, I noticed all the cardiology faculty members lined up waiting to have their pictures taken. They insisted that I have my picture taken as part of their group. I had mixed feelings. I really didn't belong there, but what was I to say? The second unexpected request was for me to "fill in" for Dr. Wooley, in making teaching rounds on his patients with his medical residents and students, because he was going to be out of town for the day. Again, I felt uneasy about the request but agreed to do so. What a great honor to have been asked! These early institutional medical experiences Dr. Wooley and I had together formed the basis for developing a close and lasting friendship until his untimely death in 2008.

This friendship was not only between the two of us, but it was also one that incorporated both of our families as well. A unique thing, however, about our close relationship was, Dr. Wooley was able to keep medical professionalism separate from friendship. It takes a master physician to accomplish that feat!

Clinical Research—A Major Training and Ongoing Assignment

During my formal training days with the Division of Cardiology at the Ohio State School of Medicine, I was invited to participate in two separate clinical research projects. My role with the first project, though quite limited, included assisting Dr. Harisios Boudulous in evaluating the benefit of *Propranolol* in patients with known ischemic heart disease. The research project included the use of the treadmill exercising machine with the intravenous injection of the isotope thallium-201. Thallium, when injected intravenously, is taken up in the muscle cells of the heart, which are perfused adequately with blood but taken up poorly in the areas of heart muscle which are perfused poorly. Preliminary results on three patients with ischemic heart disease showed that the ischemic muscle tissue of the heart perfused blood better to the area of ischemic tissue after having been on propanolol for at least forty-eight hours. It was our reasoning that since increased blood flows to the coronary arteries during diastole (relaxed phase of the heart), propanolol (a beta blocker) prolongs the diastolic phase, allowing more time for perfusion of blood to the arteries.

The second clinical research assignment was to evaluate a family whose affected members presented with significant problems of their heart, including rhythm disturbances, electrical conduction abnormalities leading to heart block, congestive heart failure, and sudden cardiac death. This formal research study began in the latter half of 1974 and continued long after my first formal retirement years in cardiology. Because of its great importance to international cardiology, more detail will be devoted to this topic in the following paragraphs.

OSU Family—Dilated Cardiomyopathy with Conduction System Disease

Dr. Wooley handed me five patient medical records, all having congestive heart failure, AV block, atrial arrhythmias (premature atrial beats and/or atrial fibrillation), and ventricular arrhythmias. He said, "I am not sure, but these patients may all be from the same family. I think this might be *familial.*" I ask him, "Where can I go to find the answer?" He replied, "There is no known answer. It will be up to you to find out." Little did I realize this research assignment would extend itself into months and years of hard work but with incomprehensible excitement and rewards.

Fortunately Dr. Wooley had been given several volumes of genealogy books of the family, whose last names bore the same as was found in the five medical records he had shared with me. A medical student had already prepared nine separate charts bearing the names of the nine second-generation siblings, including their descendants. From these medical records, a pedigree was developed. I carefully reviewed the records that were handed to me and listed all the abnormal signs and symptoms pertaining to these five patients and from their relatives that was included in the family history. The most mentioned symptoms included chest pain, shortness of breath, leg swelling, slow heart rate, irregular heart rhythm, lightheadedness, strokes, and sudden cardiac death.

A questionnaire was developed listing all the abnormal symptoms of the five affected patients and their relatives as was mentioned in the family history. A letter was constructed, explaining our interest and concern regarding the illnesses of the family members we had cared for, thinking this might represent a hereditary condition. If interested, we encouraged each of the persons to complete the questionnaire, provide a signature of consent, and return it to us. The questionnaires were mailed, and an excellent response was received. The data was reviewed and was tabulated onto the pedigree.

The next step was to invite all interested family members who had returned their questionnaires to receive a free electrocardiogram. The response was excellent. Those who had abnormal symptoms and/or abnormal electrocardiograms also received an echocardiogram. Consent was obtained to also review medical records from their family physicians' offices as well as from the Ohio State University Medical Center (both active and stored medical files). After the completion of the extensive review of medical records and interpretation of the electrocardiograms and echocardiograms, the data was reviewed and constructed onto a graphic format (pedigrees). Now we were able to better answer (1) that those initial medical records did represent members of the same family, (2) all affected members (male and female) had similar heart problems, and (3) the same heart problems occurred in each subsequent generation. From the data obtained, we were able to hypothesize (provide a tentative explanation) that the affected members of this family do have a suspected muscle and electrical tissue disease of the heart, that it does affect each subsequent generation, including male and female. Following careful review of our investigation, and review of the medical literature, we postulated (tentative explanation) that this family has an *autosomal dominant* dilated cardiomyopathy and conduction disease of the heart.

What I have provided represents a simplistic accounting of my original part of research investigation. I have included brief abstracts of three pertinent scientific publications, beginning from 1986 through 2011. The original investigation of the "OSU Family" demonstrates what the third article confirms. Our research began with a clinical suspicion from Dr. Charles F. Wooley, cardiologist, that the patients he consulted might have familial cardiac disease. This set in motion a clinical investigation that included evaluating multiple family members, leading to the hypothesis that this family had *autosomal dominant* dilated cardiopathy with conduction system disease (a suspicion backed up by pedigree, autopsy, and biopsy data). After establishing the family pedigree, examining and performing studies on the "OSU Family," the scientific data was written up in abstract form and presented at multiple scientific meetings. I was invited to be the presenter at the various meetings under the tulege of my professor, Dr. Wooley. As a starter, I presented our scientific work both locally and state levels, then the regional level—at Chicago, Illinois—next at the national level including Houston, Texas, and Atlanta, Georgia. After completing my presentation at the Houston meeting, I sat down beside my mentor, Dr. Wooley. He leaned over and whispered, "Not bad for a farm boy." Probably the greatest privilege was presenting our scientific work at the International Cardiology Meeting, which was held in Germany. This was truly a great privilege. Lastly, I was privileged to share our investigative work at the Internal Medicine Grand Rounds of the Ohio State University and the University of Virginia. One of my favorite quotations is "For every privilege, there is an equal responsibility." I assure you, I took this responsibility very seriously.

Learning to Write for Scientific Journals

Writing up the subject matter of one's investigative research is a unique and difficult task. It must be factual and use concise wording without unnecessary adjectives—knowing the subject matter is a given. Not having previous experience in writing medical articles, I enrolled in a special class to gain some important expertise. Even after completing the writing course, I felt I had hardly qualified to become an amateur writer. I don't recall how many times I was required to rewrite our first scientific paper, but it seemed to be at least twenty times. Assisting me with this assignment was the late Dr. Donald V. Unverferth, cardiologist and faculty member of Ohio State University. I will be forever grateful to him for his splendid help.

When it came time to submit our scientific paper to editors of different cardiology journals, we met up with some difficulty. The reason being, never before had anyone presented a scientific paper, claiming it to be hereditary dilated cardiomyopathy with associated conduction disease resulting from a hereditary cause. Up to this time, the *World Health Organization* recognized this type of problem to be known as *idiopathic dilated cardiomyopathy* that is, muscle disease of the heart of unknown cause. Here we were, presenting our scientific paper as being that of an inheritable cause, something that had not been described before. After multiple attempts, the editor of the heart journal, *Circulation*, accepted our work for publication in 1986. I can still hear Dr. Wooley say with excitement, "Now that's real research!" The next paragraph will include three retyped abstracts taken from published scientific papers on "OSU Family," an ongoing study since the original work, which began in 1973. These abstracts will begin to not only prove our initial hypothesis to be true, but will include the discovery of an abnormal mutation within the centromere (the horizontal "cross bar") of Chromosome I. A third abstract will describe the importance of the clinical physician to obtain an in-depth family history on all patients. When there is suspicion of a familial disease, a simple family pedigree should be constructed. If a high suspicion remains, a referral to a medical center would be in order for possible further diagnostic evaluations. This is exactly what happened with the family we studied. After constructing a pedigree of this family, we were able to see that there was a strong suspicion for a familial autosomal dominant disorder. This suspicion began with one cardiology physician, Dr. Charles F. Wooley. He, in turn, started the intellectual wheels in motion. Up to this point in time, the World Health Organization looked at this to be an *idiopathic dilated cCardiomyopathy*, meaning of unknown cause. After accumulating sufficient data from multiple generations on this family, we sought help by collaborating our efforts with Drs. Jon and Christine Steidman, geneticists at Harvard University, for further investigative studies. This required a level of genetic expertise not yet available at our institution. The Dr. Steidman team was responsible for unraveling the important nitty-gritty of this family's genetic problem. No one individual or group of persons can take sole claim for this dramatic and exciting discovery. It involved everybody working together. Because of this, the affected members of this family have benefited. Upon the completion of the basic science laboratory efforts, scientific information can now go back to the primary physician to care for his patients. Not only did this family benefit; patients around the globe will also be privileged to receive better care.

Abstract no. 1: "Evolution of a hereditary cardiac conduction and muscle disorder: a study involving a family with six generations affected"

Harry L. Graber, MD; Donald V. Unverferth, MD; Peter B. Baker, MD; Joseph M. Ryan, MD; Nobuhisa Baba, MD; and Charles F. Wooley, MD

ABSTRACT: This study describes six generations of a family with autosomal dominant cardiac conduction system and myocardial disease with recognizable clinical stages. A twenty-year follow-up of nine family members, a medical questionnaire of one hundred ninety-six, electrocardiographic screening of ninety-one, noninvasive testing of twenty, and catheterization with endomyocardial biopsy of six are the basis of this report. The clinical stages are as follows: Stage I occurs in the second and third decades of life and is characterized by an absence of symptoms, normal heart size, sinus bradycardia, and premature atrial contractions. Stage II is marked by first-degree atrioventricular block in the third and fourth decades. Stage IV, in the fifth and sixth decades of life, is characterized by congestive heart failure and recurrent ventricular arrhythmias. Light microscopy of right ventricular endomyocardial biopsy specimens from patients in stage II revealed very mild fibrosis; electron microscopy of the specimens demonstrated mild dilatation of tubules, mitochondrial swelling, and minimal myofibrillar loss. Biopsy specimens from patients with stage III disease were similar to those from patients with stage II disease except for an increase of myofibrillar loss. The stage IV specimens had diffuse fibrosis and more severe tubular dilatation, mitochondrial cristolysis, and myofibrillar loss. At autopsy in the proband (the initial patient), the atrial changes were more severe than the ventricular and were especially marked in the sinoatrial and atrial myocardium. Early recognition of the disease and use of pacemakers and antiarrhythmic agents have proved beneficial for affected family members. Thorough family studies of patients with conduction system disease and/or dilated cardiomyopathy are necessary to better understand the hereditary basis and natural course of this category of disease. *Circulation* 74, no. 1 (1986), 21–35.

Abstract no. 2: "A gene defect that causes conduction system disease and dilated cardiomyopathy maps to chromosome 1p1-1q1"

Susan Kass, Calum MacRae, Harry L. Graber, Elizabeth A. Sparks, Dennis McNamara, Harisios Boudoulas, Craig T. Basson, Peter B. Baker

III, Robert J. Cody, Mark C. Fisman, Nancy Cox, Augustine Kong, Charles F. Wooley, J. G. Seidman, and Christine E. Seidman

ABSTRACT: Longitudinal evaluation of a seven-generation kindred with an inherited conduction system defect and dilated cardiomyopathy demonstrated autosomal dominant transmission of a progressive disorder that both perturbs atrioventricular conduction and depresses cardiac contractility. To elucidate the molecular genetic basis for this disorder, a genome-wide linkage analysis was performed. Polymorphic loci near the centromere of chromosome 1 demonstrated linkage to the disease locus (maximum multipoint lod score = 13.2 in the interval between *D1S305* and *D1S176*). Based on the disease phenotype and map location, we speculate that gap junction protein connexin 40 is a candidate for mutations that result in conduction system disease and dilated cardiomyopathy.

Nature Genetics 7, August 1994, 546–551.

Abstract no. 3: "Heritable cardiac conduction and myocardial disease: from the clinic to the basic science, laboratory and back to the clinic"

Elizabeth A. Sparks, Konstantinos Dean Boudoulas, Subba V. Raman, Takeshi Sasaki, Harry L. Graber, Steven D. Nelson, Christine E. Seidman, Harisios Boudoulas

ABSTRACT: A close collaboration between the physicians-scientists of the Division of Cardiology, Ohio State University, and the basic scientists of the Department of Genetics, Harvard Medical School, was essential to define the multiple phenotypic expressions and the genetic abnormalities in the heritable conduction and myocardial disease in a family from central Ohio (OSU Family). The OSU Family study presents evidence of sequential hierarchical progression through multiple cardiac phenotypes (sinus bradycardia, atrioventricular conduction defects requiring pacemaker, supraventricular arrhythmias including atrial fibrillation, heart failure, and sudden cardiac death) on a decade-to-decade basis. In this setting, each phenotype may be mistakenly considered as a specific diagnosis by physicians working without a pedigree or long-term follow-up. Genetic analysis, however, confirms lamin A/C mutation. The role of the physician-scientist and the basic scientist in the study of heritable disorders is equally important but different. Only the physician-scientist, however, who is in constant contact with the patient understands the complexity of the disease. The physician-scientist with an interest in a particular disease can guide the basic scientist to define molecular mechanisms of that disease and by extension learn important lessons for other diseases.

Cardiology 201 (2011), 118:179–186.

I am aware that presenting the reader with the three scientific abstracts from these respective manuscripts may have been very difficult to understand, but it should bring to attention the complexity of the language we are required to use. I have shared only three of the many scientific writings that have appeared into the medical literature since the original published article of 1986. Many medical scientists have contributed in making this a success story, and the assignment is not completed. It will be a day of great celebration when lamin A/C mutation in the affected members of this family can be corrected.

During my tenure with the Ohio State University School of Medicine, I have been privileged to present our research endeavors regionally: two times at a national level and one international presentation in Germany. I was also privileged to present our study at Grand Rounds at Ohio State University as well as at the University of Virginia. Because of these great privileges, and more, I remain extremely grateful for having been taught and influenced by physicians of renowned expertise during my cardiology fellowship, plus the ensuing years that followed. Regarding the research assignment I was given upon entry of my training at Ohio State University, I remain indebted to the late Dr. Charles F. Wooley, Elizabeth A. Sparks, RN, and Drs. Jon and Christine Steidman.

As previously mentioned, becoming a physician is a continuous process. Graduating from a medical school was only a beginning for me. Now it is time to move on with my story and take us back to Mary Rutan Hospital of Bellefontaine, Ohio.

CHAPTER 7

My Return to Mary Rutan Hospital as a Cardiologist

This chapter begins with the return of one cardiologist and ends with three. It also introduces a professional relationship between the Division of Cardiology of the Ohio State University and cardiology associates of Bellefontaine, Ohio—a new and exciting adventure!

My Return to Mary Rutan Hospital

This leads me to the next part of my medical journey. I returned to Mary Rutan Hospital to put into place the *noninvasive* cardiology program, envisioned by Dr. Charles F. Wooley, et al., from the Ohio State University School of Medicine. The year was the fall of 1974. But before I begin the next chapter of my continuum in becoming a physician, reflect with me about an early concern I had. The concern was this: When I was a student at St. Louis University School of Medicine, an *infectious disease* professor had said, "If you want to practice quality medicine, you should go to a large medical center." At that time, my silent reply was, "That is your opinion." Well, providentially for me, it turned out to be a very pleasant and worthy compromise, for this was the beginning of a long-lasting relationship with Ohio State University and Mary Rutan Hospital. My future professional medical life would be incorporated into active participation at both sites, a partnership I never regretted.

I became *the vehicle* to carry out a cardiology plan, specifically designed for Mary Rutan Hospital, organized by Drs. Richard Lewis, chief of cardiology, and Charles F. Wooley from the Division of Cardiology at Ohio State University. They were confident that I would be able to interpret electrocardiograms, perform and interpret exercise stress tests and echocardiograms, Holter-monitor recordings of patients' heart rhythms, and, later on, include nuclear stress testing and interpretation. While I felt quite comfortable with the proposed plan, soon there were several hurdles to overcome: (1) A number of family physicians had been interpreting their own electrocardiograms as well as for other physicians. Was this an issue for discussion? Not really. I saw no reason to suggest making any changes for the present time. (2) A second hurdle to overcome was initiated by physicians who were not affiliated with Oakhill Medical Associates. I was informed, that to be a true cardiology consultant for the entire medical community, I would need to become independent from Oakhill Medical Associates. (3) The last hurdle was a cost factor. The cost of the proposed equipment for a basic cardiology department at Mary Rutan Hospital was almost prohibitive. I wrestled over these three problems at great length.

The first problem, regarding who may formally interpret electrocardiograms, was quite easy to resolve. I would not attempt to recommend a change. I weighed the second problem very carefully, then concluded that I should make my cardiology services available to all physicians of the medical community. With that decision, I left Oakhill Medical Associates and established my temporary office in the basement of Mary Rutan Hospital. Shortly afterward, the third hurdle was also solved. Soon after returning to the Bellefontaine community, I received a phone call from one of my patients. He apologetically asked me to see an elderly neighbor lady whom I had never seen before. She was experiencing progressive shortness of breath and had pronounced swelling of her legs. He also added her mental status was deteriorating. I immediately went to the patient's home. It didn't take long to realize the patient was in severe congestive heart failure, requiring immediate hospitalization. Unfortunately, she soon expired. Unknown until later, this lady was a daughter of a physician who had formally practiced medicine in the community years ago. After her death, a sizable sum of money was given to the new cardiology department of the hospital. Soon after that event, another gentleman of the community committed a large sum of money to the hospital and to be used by the cardiology department. Hence, my first three hurdles were solved.

Not long after my return to Mary Rutan Hospital, it was suggested that a year of cardiology doesn't make one a cardiologist. I was in complete agreement; besides, Dr. Lewis had asked me to stay at Ohio State University to complete the recommended two-year cardiology training program. As a result of the advice I was given, I spent the next one and one-half years alternating working at Mary Rutan Hospital and returning to OSU to complete the required cardiology fellowship program. Most of this educational time was spent gaining more expertise in nuclear cardiology and electrophysiology (developing catheterization skills and learning more about the electrical functions of the heart). In addition, I attended all the required educational meetings and continued my work with my research assignment. During my time intervals spent at OSU, two internal medicine specialists provided coverage for me at Mary Rutan Hospital.

Finally, in 1979, my cardiology fellowship training was completed. By this time, all the physicians at Mary Rutan Hospital had accepted the concept of having a formally trained cardiologist within the community. It wasn't long until I became extremely busy and was in need of help. Besides delivering full-time cardiology service to the patients at Mary Rutan Hospital, I spent every Thursday, my day off, at Ohio State University continuing my research on heritable dilated cardiomyopathy.

A Plea for Help

In 1980, I received a welcomed call from my dear friend and colleague, Dr. Wooley, who said he thinks he had found somebody to join me in cardiology at Mary Rutan Hospital. His name was Evan Dixon, MD, who was just finishing his cardiology fellowship at OSU. Prior to his training in cardiology, Dr. Dixon had been an instructor at Ohio University medical school of Athens, Ohio, as a pulmonary specialist (lung specialist). Before this, he served as chief medical resident at OSU. Dr. Wooley said he thought Dr. Dixon would be a perfect fit for me at Bellefontaine. With that impressive background information, I called Dr. Dixon. I mentioned I had recently completed my cardiology training at Ohio State University and was looking for a partner and that his name was given to me by Dr. Charles Wooley. I stated, if interested, I would like to meet with him and give him a tour of our hospital. He accepted my invitation. After a tour of the hospital, we went to our newly constructed office building to chat and discuss my proposed plans in more detail. Dr. Wooley had already explained how OSU had envisioned and helped to make the Mary Rutan Hospital cardiology facility become a reality. I stated I was interested in having him consider my invitation to join me and to let me know if he had any other questions. I also informed him that he was highly recommended to me by Dr. Charles Wooley, whom we both knew quite well. It wasn't long afterward that Dr. Dixon called and accepted my generous offer.

It didn't take long to learn that Dr. Dixon and I shared many important values in common. We were both raised on a farm; therefore, we were not afraid of work. We were both perfectionists and therefore demanded high standards. We both had our patients at heart; our purpose was to provide quality medical service and care for our patients. We were both teachers of medicine. We also had the same weakness: we created more work than we could handle. Within a period of two years, we were begging for more help.

Dr. Evan Dixon

Dr. Dixon was one of three physicians to receive the distinguished resident alumnus award from The Ohio State University Medical Center. It was the first year the awards were presented. Dr. Dixon was honored for his commitment to education and training programs at the medical center. He has been a cardiologist in Bellefontaine since 1982 and has been responsible for the expansion of the nuclear and peripheral vascular programs.

Dr. Evan Dixon

1982—A Need for Additional Help

In addition to seeing inpatients and outpatients in consultation for their heart problems, Dr. Dixon and I were currently performing and evaluating the following studies of the heart: stress exercise studies, echocardiograms, Holter-monitoring of heart rhythms, electrocardiograms, implanting pacemakers, and soon to include nuclear stress testing. Because of a time factor, we were contemplating to discontinue the invasive study of electrophysiology. We definitely were in need of some professional help. Dr. Dixon came up with a great idea to arrange a one-day workshop at

Mary Rutan Hospital to seek expert advice in how to plan and organize our newly established cardiology department. We did not want to compromise the quality of our professional services to our patients. We were seeking honest opinions and recommendations from an outside professional source. A site visit was organized, inviting physicians from three separate medical institutions. Included were: Dr. Peter Temesy-Armos, Medical College of Ohio at Toledo; Drs. John Robinson, and Charles Wooley, Ohio State University; Dr. Robert Murane, Mt. Carmel Medical Center, Columbus, Ohio. Members from Mary Rutan Hospital were Mrs. Connie Rhodes, director of cardiology; Drs. Graber and Dixon; and Mr. Ewing H. Crawfis, administrator of Mary Rutan Hospital. Following a tour of the department, a detailed discussion was held, and recommendations were later received by mail.

The visiting professors were very complimentary with the cardiology division at Mary Rutan Hospital. Some felt this could become a regional medical facility. One professor felt it reasonable to consider a more formal working agreement or relationship with the Ohio State University Hospitals. Another professor suggested bringing in other specialty groups along with another cardiologist. All agreed there was need for at least one more cardiologist. The site visit was very exciting and extremely helpful. The workshop proved to be timely and of extreme importance. It motivated us to (1) acquire a third cardiologist, (2) pave the way for a closer association with the Division of Cardiology of Ohio State University, and (3) bring in other subspecialty and primary care physicians, as recommended by the visiting physician consultants. As you read on, you will note that all three of the recommendations made by the "on-site professionals" were put into action.

1984—Third Cardiologist Recruited

It was the spring of 1984, when I attended the *Heart House*, headquarters of the American College of Cardiology at Bethesda, Maryland, for an educational meeting. Whom did I see, but Dr. Vincent Petno, a cardiologist from the Medical Center of Akron, General Hospital of Akron, Ohio. Dr. Petno and I both received our postgraduate training there in internal medicine. We spent valuable time catching up with each other's recent years of professional activities. As we were reminiscing, I was asked how things were going at Bellefontaine, Ohio. When I mentioned our need for a third cardiologist, he was in disbelief how a small town such as

Bellefontaine, Ohio, would need a third person, let alone having the two of us already there. I told him of all the procedures we were already doing and were desperately looking for a third partner. The subject was dropped for the time being. Sometime later, the topic of cardiology need was brought up again. I repeated that we were very busy, and we could use a third full-time cardiologist. I sensed he might be interested, so I suggested that he and his wife come to Bellefontaine to visit us. The initial conversation between the two of us was also shared with our wives and Dr. Dixon. It was not long after that arrangements were made, and Dr. Petno and his wife, Lee, came to visit us to get a firsthand look at our facility, meet my associate Dr. Dixon, and tour the town. It wasn't long after that we received a positive response from my friend, Dr. Petno, that he and his family were moving to Bellefontaine, Ohio, to join us in our practice of cardiology. I didn't know this at the time, but later, Dr. Petno mentioned that I was his mentor when he trained at Akron General.

Dr. Petno had outstanding credentials. He received his *cardiology fellowship* training at the Cleveland Clinic and was currently serving as a cardiologist at the Akron General Medical Center of Akron, Ohio. He was currently the director of cardiac function, pacemaker, and cardiac rehabilitation departments. Looking back, the gathering of two friends at the *Heart House* proved to be more than an important historic visit. It was providential that Dr. Petno and Dr. Dixon, both with coveted credentials and character, should come to join me at Mary Rutan Hospital of Bellefontaine, Ohio. What a team! Although of different physical traits and personalities, we all three had received excellent training, claimed similar spiritual values, dedication, and eagerness to work together and work for a common cause: "to care for our patients."

Providing excellent care for our patients was of foremost importance to all three of us. Dr. Petno was gifted as an organizer with administrative skills. He had in-depth experience in establishing both pacemaker and cardiac rehabilitation clinics. Dr. Dixon was quite gifted in general cardiology and pulmonary medicine and was knowledgeable in selecting quality brands of cardiology equipment. My extracurricular interests included ongoing research and education for my patients. Having been a former schoolteacher, I wanted to make sure my patients had a clear understanding of their problem and the reason for the treatment they were to receive. I fell in love with both gentlemen and offered them compensation equal to mine. We became a great team! As expected, with the quality of these two gentlemen, as individuals and their training experience, the cardiology department of Mary Rutan Hospital continued to flourish and expand.

Dr. Dixon already had the nuclear exercise testing laboratory in place and functioning well. It wasn't long after Dr. Petno's arrival that both the new pacemaker clinic and the cardiac rehabilitation center were set up and functioning well. Although both of these facilities were started before his arrival, his professional expertise and directorship were greatly needed and appreciated. Looking back, if there was any accomplishment I wished to be noted for, it was that I helped bring two outstanding cardiologists to Mary Rutan Hospital of Bellefontaine, Ohio.

Vincent Petno, M.D., Cardiologist,
new associate joining Drs. Graber and Dixon.

1987—Invitation to Join Cardiology Faculty of Ohio State University

Although Dr. Dixon and I were already considered faculty members of the Division of Cardiology at the Ohio State University School of Medicine, this invitation was to formally invite the three of us to become salaried faculty members with assistant clinical professorship status.

This would now make us clinical medical staff members of Ohio State University, in addition to our medical staff membership with Mary Rutan Hospital. The acceptance of this offer would open the door for medical residents and cardiology fellows to rotate through Mary Rutan Hospital, providing they chose to do so. This rotational program for cardiology fellows became a reality and added excitement for our teaching staff. It also opened the door for other postdoctorate physicians and students to rotate through our hospital. Later on, a postgraduate residency program in family medicine was established under the directorship of Dr. Randall Longenecker. This, too, became a cooperative adventure between Mary Rutan and the Ohio State University Hospitals. The growth and expansion of the Mary Rutan Hospital Cardiology Department, as well as the other subspecialty groups, continued to progress and so did its reputation. Word had spread that for a hospital its size, it had the best cardiology department within the state of Ohio.

The years went by rapidly. By 1990, Dr. Glen Miller, internal medicine specialist and medical director of the hospital, retired and I succeeded him to become its medical director from 1990 to 1999. This created a need to find a new replacement for cardiology associates. This position was soon filled by recruiting William Houser, MD, a well-trained young cardiologist from the University of Cincinnati, Ohio. He received his medical school training at the Ohio State University. Dr. Petno retired in 1997 after spending thirteen years with us in Bellefontaine, Ohio. His outstanding contributions to this medical community will long be remembered. Replacing him was my son, Rodney L. Graber, MD, who also completed his cardiology training at Ohio State University, to join Cardiology Associates in July 1999. Shortly after this, the cardiology group became known as *Cardiology Associates of Ohio State University at Bellefontaine, Ohio.*

Reflecting back over the previous chapters, one can sense there is a common thread of multiple past experiences relating to the fact that the profession of medicine does indeed present itself as a continuum. Eventually, following one's retirement, the baton is passed on to a younger and better informed generation. They, too, have been touched by certain unique *environmental factors*, be it a person or some earlier life experience, beckoning him/her to become a physician. As for "the positive turnaround" of Mary Rutan Hospital, the physician with the original dream was the late Paul Hooley, MD. He had a vision of developing a medical clinic, which in turn brought into the community young physicians of the most recent education. They too had a dream, one that helped revolutionize the status quo of the "old" into a modern medical community and hospital facility that is recognized among the best. I am thankful I remained in Logan County, Ohio, and could be a part of this progress story. To gain a better perspective of what I have written, the next chapter will take the reader back to the late 1960s and 1970s. This will provide some necessary insight what Mary Rutan Hospital was perceived to be during that era. It will also introduce how feelings of discontent were transformed into positive action: a true success story.

CHAPTER 8

Who Is Mary Rutan and Why Does She Keep Sending These Patients?

This chapter addresses the above question that was asked by a medical resident physician at Ohio State University some years ago. It also touches upon some early problems that were perceived by physicians at about the time of my entry into the Bellefontaine, Ohio, community and how these problems were successfully dealt with. This chapter also presents updates on improvements and expansion of Mary Rutan Hospital starting from the late 1960s to the present time. But first of all, "Who is Mary Rutan and Why Does She Keep Sending These Patients?"

Who Is Mary Rutan?

This question was asked one Monday morning by a medical resident physician from Ohio State University Medical Center who happened to be on call on a given weekend. It was the cover article of *Up/Date,* an Ohio State publication that was handed out to hospitals belonging to the *Health Care Consortium of Ohio.* The medical resident thought it appropriate to write the question on the chalkboard as he was about to share the weekend patient admissions. Apparently a number of those patient admissions had come from Mary Rutan Hospital of Bellefontaine, Ohio. What the *physician* did not know, and perhaps what others do not know, the patient referral pattern from Mary Rutan Hospital to Ohio State University Medical Center represents a by-product of hard work that had been going on between the two institutions. It was the beginning of a professional relationship that was initiated between the two medical communities, starting from the mid- to late 1970s. The above question "Who is Mary Rutan?" seems quite appropriate and deserves a reasonable answer, so let us start from the beginning.

Picture of Mary Magruder Rutan
(1st hospital named after her per request of Her daughter)

Mary Rutan Hospital came into existence in 1919, through a bequest of Rebecca Rutan Williams. Mrs. Williams left proceeds from the family farm located near Ridgeway, Ohio, to the city of Bellefontaine. The money was designated for the purpose of constructing a hospital to be built and named in honor of her mother, Mary Magruder Rutan. The original hospital was 7,800 square feet and could accommodate twenty-four patients but had the potential of serving an additional eleven patients in the case of an emergency. Because the property was given to the city of Bellefontaine, all hospital trustees were to be elected from within the city. As I look back at its beginning, the hospital was a small structure but served the community quite well. In sequence to the original hospital structure, multiple changes and additions have occurred over a period of many decades, but not without its problems and challenges. One of the problems that was recognized and dealt with occurred during the late 1960s and 1970s. The next several paragraphs will include brief updates of these historical changes.

Original Hospital, named Mary Rutan Hospital 1919

Hospital Environment During the 1960s and 1970s

Upon arriving to my first place of work at Mary Rutan Hospital of Logan County, Ohio, I came to the community with much excitement! As might be true with many newcomers, being fresh out of training from a large medical teaching center, I had very little insight of what to expect. Except for size differences, I envisioned most hospitals as being comparable to each other. But this was not the case. The physical structure and medical equipment within this hospital appeared to be outdated. The laboratory was quite small and had a limited number of laboratory tests available for assisting the physician in managing the patient. There was no on-site pathologist but one who came from another city from time to time. The emergency room was extremely small and limited in necessary equipment. From the perspective of a young medical "whipper-snapper" like me, the setting was not very impressive. I really didn't know if I wanted to be here. I kept thinking about that large medical center I was invited to in South Bend, Indiana. To add to my frustration, one day a physician staff member stopped to talk to me in the hallway. During the conversation, he said, "Nothing new has happened in medicine in the past ten years." I thought to myself, *That may be true for you, but I have news for you.* To add to my negative assessment, certain patients would tell me that Mary Rutan Hospital was just a "shoebox." At this point, one may wonder, why didn't I move away from this place? Well, one very good reason was I had learned there were some very fine people whom I met in Logan County. Not long afterward, I began to fall in love with the people of this community, so I began to change my attitude. I began to wonder, maybe, *just maybe, other hospitals of similar size, from other rural medical communities might be comparable to Mary Rutan Hospital.* I reflected, thinking how medicine was practiced in larger medical centers during the same time frame. A few of these reflections will be shared in the next paragraph.

Pacemakers were just being introduced at medical centers. I'm not sure I witnessed any implanted where I had received my training in Akron, Ohio. I do recall one lady being externally paced at the St. Louis Medical Center on a surgical ward in 1963. The battery was quite large and had coated wires attached externally to the patient's chest. It did not have the capabilities to sense the patient's own rhythm, thus creating a potential problem of inducing an abnormal arrhythmia. I also recall during my medical residency training days that certain cardiologists were routinely using Warfarin on all their patients with sustained acute heart attacks. These patients were kept at bed rest for several weeks before increasing their activities. I also remember we were not permitted to order electrolytes from the laboratory during the night without obtaining approval from the pathologist—this was also true for weekends. All these historical practice memories became refreshed in my mind. So what was it that I was disturbed about? I'm not sure, but I did feel there were some deficiencies about the Mary Rutan Hospital that were worth discussing. I shared my concerns with my new colleague, Dr. Glen Miller, and he was just as disturbed as I was. As it turned out, there were others who felt the same. Based upon our observations, three major problems existed. There appeared to be a qualitative deficiency within the framework of the hospital building. Second, the administrative leadership did not appear to be adequately equipped for their assignment. Third, it would seem exceedingly difficult to experience positive changes as long as the hospital was kept under the rule of the city of Bellefontaine, for it appeared to be a political operation. These concerns formed the basis for presenting our concerns formally to the medical staff.

Though a difficult task, a medical staff meeting was held, and the three basic concerns were brought to everyone's attention. The majority of the medical staff was in agreement of the first two issues regarding a deficiency of the hospital structure and administrative leadership, but the third concern was more complicated to deal with. After several special meetings, including help from legal council, the way was paved to pursue a long-term lease from the city of Bellefontaine, allowing the hospital to become a *community hospital*. Although these were monumental issues to tackle, it paved the way for great positive changes for the hospital community of Bellefontaine, Ohio.

Ewing H. Crawfis Hospital Administrator
of Mary Rutan (1977-2004)

The time was ripe to begin searching for a fully trained hospital administrator. After interviewing several prospective hospital administrators, we made a selection to offer the administrative assignment to a young gentleman who was well educated and versed in hospital administrative matters. His name was Mr. Ewing H. Crawfis, assistant administrator at Community Hospital of Springfield, Ohio. He accepted the offer, and this proved to be an outstanding find! The year was 1977. It didn't require much time for Mr. Crawfis to review the existing internal and external environment of the hospital, present recommendations to the newly elected hospital board of trustees and medical staff, and seek approval of those recommendations. Though much time was required, we were not only off to a good start but also experienced the beginning of a complete overhaul of the medical staff bylaws and the restructuring of the hospital board of directors. It also was the beginning of attracting new physicians to the community. This included both family physicians and specialists, with the immediate need to find a full-time pathologist and radiologist. Although many persons contributed to this project, Dr. Glen Miller and Dr. James McGriff are to be congratulated for their input, playing important and leading roles in bringing about these early positive changes for Mary Rutan Hospital. Other contributing physicians included: Doctors Paul Hooley, Douglas Beach, James Steiner, Krajewsky, Arnaldo Roldan and Arthur Costin, all from family medicine; Doctors Michael Failor and Jack Ferron, emergency medicine; Doctors George Horot and Allen Stuckey, pediatrics; Doctor Grant Varian, internal medicine; Doctor John Columbo, anesthesiology; Doctors George Ginsemer, David Miller, and Charles Barrett, general surgery; Doctor Josip Terebuh, ophthalmology; Doctor Koo Moon, urology; Doctors Jeffrey Barrows and Jay Meyer, obstetrics/gynecology; Doctor Thomas Franklin, orthopedic surgery; Doctor Donald Leese, radiology; Doctors Kim and Robert Davis, pathology and Doctor Harry Graber, cardiology.

Years later, all but one of the originally named physicians have handed their *batons* on to younger professionals with updated training to represent the different specialties. There was not one person who could claim special recognition for this early success story. All were committed toward achieving a common goal: to provide the best medical care for the people of Logan County. Added to the above-listed specialties now included pain management, neurology, psychiatry, otolaryngology, rheumatology and nephrology, the latter two being provided as outside consultants.

Newest Addition of Mary Rutan Hospital

Mandy Goble CEO of Mary Rutan Hospital (2004-present)

In 1989, Mandy Goble became vice president of operations of Mary Rutan Hospital. From 1989 to 2004, she was involved in the development and opening of some of the following departments and services: Corporate Health Services, Sleep Laboratory, Audiology Services, Cardiac Catheterization Lab; CT/MRI Services; upgrading of the Pediatric Department; Mad River Internal Medicine; Obstetrics/Gynecology; and Mad River Family Practice.

From 1995 through 2008, Mandy Goble oversaw the expansions and renovations of the new obstetrics labor and delivery unit, the new surgery, new ICCU, and major renovations to the existing facility. She also oversaw the renovation of the Emergency Department in 2008, increasing it from 3,300 to 17,500 square feet; the construction of the Rehabilitation Center (12,000 square feet) for physical and occupational therapies, Speech and Audiology Services, the construction of the Imaging Center, and the construction and opening of the Regional Cancer Center, which later became the Ambulatory Care Center.

Following the death of Mr. Ewing Crawfis in 2004, Mrs. Goble became and continues to serve as the CEO of Mary Rutan Hospital. Under her auspices, the one-hundred-bed hospital, which employs more than one hundred physicians and seven hundred employees, was awarded the *Outstanding Patient Experience Award* for the third straight year since 2012, placing it among the top 10 percent of hospitals in the USA.

Several decades have gone by since that *medical resident physician* asked, "Who is Mary Rutan?" Many positive changes have occurred, thanks to many individuals who relentlessly gave of themselves to advise, initiate, and assist in the construction of a great community healthcare institution known as *Mary Rutan Hospital*. One person's dream, set into action, provided the necessary cornerstone for others to build upon. Although the tools used for construction have changed, the message has clearly remained the same: "To provide the best health care for every person of Logan County." Many individuals of the past have dedicated themselves to carry out this single and most important objective. We have witnessed a legacy of excellence under the leadership of the late Ewing Crawfis in providing the healthcare needs for this community, one that has been difficult to match. In addition to his leadership, he had mentored another outstanding leader, Mandy Goble, currently carrying that administrative banner, meeting the health needs of the present and into the next generation.

What has been presented is a remarkable success story for our community hospital, thanks to the excellent leadership of our administration, hospital boards, members of all medical and nursing staffs, and all employees of

Mary Rutan Hospital. All have worked long and hard in providing a medical service of excellence for this community. The lesson to be learned is "When dissatisfaction arises, don't leave or sit around complaining about it, but look for solutions to correct the problem." It was my privilege to have been an active participant in making these improvements happen. The positive improvements that have happened to this medical community is also inclusive in the making of a physician.

The Initiation of Medical Education for the Medical Staff and Community

Leadership in medical education is another area of responsibility that incorporates *the making of the physician*. Having been in the profession of education in the public school systems, I find it important to teach my patients and help organize ongoing medical education for physicians and the community. The *first goal* included spending quality time with my patients in providing them a better understanding of their medical problems, stating the reason for prescribing their medications, and explaining the importance for adhering to an appropriate lifestyle. This often required extended time in caring for them. My routine was to spend one hour with every new patient and one-half hour with every follow-up patient. A *second goal* was to help develop quality educational programs for physicians that would merit CME (continued medical education) credit for ongoing medical education (a requirement for maintaining an active medical license), locally as well as from a university setting. The *third goal* was to provide an educational opportunity for citizens of the Logan County community. More discussion will be required for the last two goals.

Medical Education at the Local Level

The first medical educational meetings were held in a room next to the hospital cafeteria. They occurred in the morning before the start of the physicians' workday, on a monthly basis. The initial meetings were very informal. Attendance was not mandatory. Those choosing to participate would take turns in discussing a topic of his/her choice. I remember one physician shared the scientific basis for manipulative treatment of a patient with back pain. This was new but quite interesting and informative for me. As time went on, meetings became more formal and didactic. This was particularly true with the required attendance of the monthly mortality conference. This conference included a review of all patient deaths for a given month. The routine protocol was to just check to make sure that appropriate care was given to the deceased patients. To make it more interesting and worthwhile, we began to select a deceased case that we felt would be of special interest for teaching purposes. On a rotational basis, the assigned physician would be responsible to review the deceased patient's medical record in depth, review the medical literature relating to that patient's problem, and present the case to the medical staff. This brought a new level of interest to the mortality conference, and they became quite educational. As the medical education concept progressed, we began to include patients with complex or unusual medical or surgical problems and invite outside speakers from a larger medical institution to come and discuss the given case with us. This provided us with expertise from an outside source of how the patient may have been treated. For example, a patient presented with upper gastrointestinal bleeding. The patient was elderly and was prescribed nonsteroidal pain medicines (such as *Ibuprofen*). This turned out to be a very interesting and important topic for discussion. It brought to our attention that an elderly person is at increased risk for upper intestinal bleeding when taking the medicine for a prolonged period of time. Since medical problems like this mostly involves the nursing staff, we began to involve them also.

As time went on, the question became, what could the medical staff of Mary Rutan Hospital do to qualify us to receive CME credits for certain quality educational programs, presented by a local medical staff member? The answer was, the local speaker must have a formal affiliation with an institution that is accredited to provide CME credits. Being associated with Ohio State University, I was given the title of assistant clinical professor of medicine with the Division of Cardiology. Because of this formal affiliation, I was asked to serve on the CME Committee (continuing medical education) at Ohio State University—one of the purposes of that committee was to review and approve all medical educational programs originating out of the university. As a committee member, it helped pave the way toward receiving CME credit for some of our monthly medical education meetings held at Mary Rutan Hospital (MRH). Being the medical director of MRH at the time, it became my responsibility to select special topics and speakers from OSU or from any university that also had a recognized CME program. The same principle held true for any local speaker who held a formal affiliation with OSU. This became a milestone for physician educational programs at our local hospital. But it did not solve the problem of receiving CME credits when having local speakers who had no affiliation with an accredited university, no matter how outstanding he or she would be.

For some time, Dr. Robert Davis, pathologist at Mary Rutan Hospital, had been preparing outstanding case presentations for the hospital on a monthly basis. This conference not only included physicians from MRH but also those from neighboring communities as well. It also included interested nurses. Since I was still serving on the CME committee at the university, I was able to recommend Dr. Davis to become a member of the faculty of the Pathology Department of OSU. This would qualify the physicians of Mary Rutan Hospital to receive educational credit for these monthly meetings too. With Dr. Davis's credentials, the university was pleased to have him with the Division of Pathology. This turned out to be a tremendous accomplishment. We were now able to enjoy his exciting conferences and receive CME credits.

Continuing Medical Education, etc

For a number of years, Ohio State University has provided special educational programs to its constituency. Many hospitals can be tuned into this weekly network, called OMEN (Ohio Medical Education Network). At Mary Rutan, physicians are also able to attend conferences presented by OSU in internal medicine and obstetrics/gynecology and receive CME credit.

All the educational programs that have been mentioned are of great interest and importance to the physicians at Mary Rutan Hospital. A physician may earn enough CME credits by attending these sessions without needing to go elsewhere. It has been my pleasure in providing a part of the initial efforts for this postgraduate educational adventure. Dr. Grant Varian, current medical director, chairs the ongoing responsibility for these outstanding programs.

Picture of the late Shirley West, R.N.;
the late Rev. Howard Schmidt; and Dr. Harry Graber.

Professional Medical Education for the Community

It is quite unusual for physicians to provide formal health education programs to a general population of people within a given community. The only time I had previously done this type of thing was when I had shared the "OSU Family" study at one of their large family reunions. What I am presently about to share was a most uncommon adventure.

During early autumn of 1978, I was approached by the late Reverend Howard Schmidt, who asked me to arrange a series of Sunday night lectures on the topic of *coronary artery disease*. He indicated this would be an appropriate Christian education endeavor serving as an educational outreach for the entire community of Logan County. Reverend Schmidt was pastor of the South Union Mennonite Church and a clerical counselor at Mary Rutan Hospital. Besides his primary church leadership responsibilities, he was much interested in promoting Christian education beyond the confines of his congregation. He was a very visionary individual. He suggested the topic of coronary artery disease because it affects so many people, not only in Logan County, but throughout the United States as well. He said, "After all, the Bible teaches us that our bodies are *'temples of God.'* He was troubled about people with their careless health habits. With that background, he began to say, "How would it be if we would plan to have a series of lectures on *coronary artery disease* and present these to the community of Logan County?" Then, Reverend Schmidt asked if I would be responsible for initiating such a program. Although I had never done this sort of thing before, the idea was very appealing, because it is very important how we treat our bodies. I had been telling my heart patients about this epidemic problem many times, but it had not occurred to me to publicly address the subject to the Logan County community. I told Reverend Schmidt I would discuss this with a few of my colleagues but assured him the answer would most likely be affirmative.

What a coincidence! About this same time, the Central Ohio Heart Association Board (COHAB) were asking for local heart chapters to initiate programs that would help educate communities on the risks of coronary artery disease. As an incentive, they indicated the local heart chapter that developed the best program would be honored by the Central Ohio Heart Board. The fact that I was currently serving on the COHAB and was also active with the local chapter created much excitement within the local heart chapter.

A delegated group of four interested physicians met with me to put together nine specific topics related to coronary artery disease. We invited certain interested local physicians to participate in preparing and leading a discussion on their assigned topic. We asked that they included a typewritten copy of their lecture to be forwarded to a representative of the *Bellefontaine Examiner*, who would be in attendance of each meeting. The editor of the *Examiner* had agreed to print out each presentation, including pictures. This way, people of the community who could not attend the lecture series would be able to become educated by reading the local newspaper. All meetings were to be held at the South Union Mennonite Church for nine consecutive Sunday evenings, from seven thirty to eight thirty p.m. It was to be announced that everybody interested in attending these sessions were welcome to attend. The following paragraph will include the speakers with their assigned topics and will also include some of the content of the presentations.

TOPIC: "Coronary Artery Disease"
Dates: September 17–November 19, 1978
Place: South Union Mennonite Church
Time: 7:30 p.m.–8:30 p.m.
Speakers and Topics:

Dr. Harry Graber, "Introduction, Statistics on Cardiovascular Disease and Risk Factors," September 17

Dr. Harry Graber, "Epidemiological Studies on Coronary Artery Disease (International and National)," September 24

Dr. Glen Miller, "Physiology of Heart Symptoms, Diagnosis and Treatment of Coronary Artery Disease," October 1

Dr. Grant Varian, "Process of 'Hardening of Arteries,' Implications of Lipoproteins (Cholesterol and Triglycerides), Implication of Other Risk Factors," October 8

Dr. George Horst, "Diet in the Prevention and Treatment of Coronary Artery Disease," October 15

Drs. Arnaldo Roldan and James Steiner "Life Style for Mankind and Patient with Coronary Disease," October 22 Dr. Paul Hooley, "Psychological and Spiritual Role in the Treatment of Coronary Disease." October 29

Gene Esch and Steve Billiar, Paramedics, "Role of the Paramedic in the Treatment of the Heart Attack Victim." November 12

Dr. Harry Graber, "Recent Research from the American Heart Association's Writer Forum." (1978) November 19

Selected Quotes:

Coronary artery disease occurs in epidemic proportions in the United States and has been brought on mostly by a careless style of living.

Consistently, groups of clinically normal people in less developed countries, who ingested mostly vegetarian diets low in cholesterol, saturated fats, and calories had significantly lower levels of serum cholesterol than those of industrialized sectors such as the United States.

The major risk factors for coronary artery disease are heredity, hypercholesterolemia, hypertension, cigarette smoking, obesity, and diabetes.

According to Dr. Roldan, jogging is a natural tranquilizer. It allows time for meditation, discipline and closeness to nature."

According to Galen Esch and Steve Billiar, paramedics, "Of the 650,000 Americans who die of a heart attack each year, about 350,000 die before they reach the hospital, and one-third of those before the emergency squad arrives. Many expire because by-standers have never learned cardiopulmonary resescitation (CPR).

The above quotes were from the scheduled speakers in 1978 and published by the Bellefontaine *Examiner* staff writer, Erika Fiske. Thank you, Erika and the *Bellefontaine Examiner*. All these lectured presentations were well accepted by the community. Attendance averaged more than two hundred persons each night.

Educational Program for Prospective Healthcare Workers

During my clinical years as a physician, I held it in high esteem to give my best for my patients. I learned early on that "the best care I could give my patient was to care for that patient." But besides that important virtue, I also became interested in assisting young adults to fulfill their dreams, sometimes by a letter of encouragement, other times by providing a gift. I was particularly interested in seeking out those whom I thought might be become candidates for future healthcare providers—I have never forgotten how somebody sought me out during my early educational adventures, providing me with a financial gift to help fulfill my dream.

During the early to mid-1970s, I began providing a salary for students interested in a future healthcare career. I could only provide for one student's summer hospital employment at a time. This later became a program formally adopted by the hospital administration. As a result of this effort, more than ten students entered the healthcare profession. One happened to be my son, Dr. Rodney L. Graber, cardiologist. Several in this group will be sharing their story later.

CHAPTER 9

The Making of a Physician—But What About the Family?

Front row: Rodney, Charles; Back row: Rhonda, myself, Roberta, Cheryl

It's so easy to become so unintentionally involved in one's professional calling, that the family suffers the consequences of neglect. Here is my story.

Up to this point, telling my story about the making of a physician has been done with considerable satisfaction and success. However, what about the responsibility of a physician also being a husband and father to one's wife and four children? Reflecting upon those years, I sometimes feel they may have been shortchanged. Maybe so, but when a physician is required to spend sixty-plus hours per week caring for the sick, it doesn't give much time left for the family. This environmental characteristic is particularly true for those physicians with families living and working in rural communities. It is interesting how indelible these memories remain in one's mind, even at age eighty-four. Here are three vivid examples. I still owe my son Rodney a canoe trip, which I promised but never happened because I was called back to the hospital to care for a severely ill patient. Still fresh in my mind was a note I found on my bedside stand, left by one of my daughters who were leaving for college. The printed note read, "I love you, Dad, but I hardly know you." As I write, a third memory pops up to my consciousness. It had to do about weekend hospital rounds. Since I spent more Sundays at the local hospital than I wish to recall, my wife, Roberta, and the four children would meet me at the hospital for lunch. When I would arrive to meet them at the cafeteria, I would see Roberta with the children, all standing in a row, quietly waiting for me to arrive. The children were always excited because they equated this experience as eating at the "Mary Rutan Restaurant," and also, they could see their daddy. Although I remained dedicated and faithful to my calling throughout my medical career, such memories remain close to my heart, with a question in my mind as to how I might have done it a better way. Can you, the reader, imagine what impact this type of environmental atmosphere might have had on a given family, day in and day out? I don't know, but I still wonder. Our experience was not exceptional. No doubt there have been many families who, like Roberta, put their professional goals on hold to fulfill their roles of motherhood with dedication and pride. They accepted *motherhood* as their calling, only to later *witness the fruits of their labor*, which was the joy of raising their children. Not all mothers have the privilege I just mentioned, because they need to work to provide for the family. Special arrangements become necessary in such instances, to help love and care for the children. Therefore, future healthcare professionals, give careful thought when you consider medicine as your vocation. Here is my advice: the decision should be based upon a strong desire in caring for the sick. I choose to call this type of decision-making *a calling*.

If you think I have overwhelmed you with the downside of medical life, let me share how I worked through this problem. First and foremost, if you plan on being married, find a soul mate who is in complete agreement with your calling. This is an important prerequisite. If your partner is not in complete harmony with your calling, I advise discontinuing the relationship before marriage. As an example, before meeting my wife, I had been dating a very fine lady, one who was a nurse and of great moral character. However, when asked whether she felt I should pursue medicine or remain in the education profession, she thought it best to stay in education. I could tell by her response that she was not very excited about my entering medical school. That relationship soon ended, not because of my dislike for her as a person but because I felt there might be a future problem should I choose medicine as my profession. It is imperative for two people who are planning a lifetime partnership together that both be completely supportive of each other. This is how it was for Roberta, my wife for nearly fifty years. Allow me to share how we planned our life together.

Roberta and I shared many common values. We were both of Judeo-Christian faith. We were both schoolteachers with athletic interests. She had an excellent background and experience with finances and secretarial work. She was very trustworthy. Because of her expertise with budgeting, she handled all our financial matters (she might have been a little too frugal at times, but not a bad complaint for one to have). We were interdependent (mutually dependent on each other). We had similar understandings on discipline issues, and we had complete trust for one another. Roberta did have one unusual trait. She did not wish to be known as "Dr. Graber's wife." By that she meant she did not want special privileges given to her just because her husband was a physician. While she wanted to claim that independence, she would defend me at any cost! She was outgoing and became involved with many community activities. Not perfect, but close to it.

Because of my extremely busy schedule, Roberta practically raised our four children, which included two girls and two boys. She did an outstanding job! She taught them how to become dependable workers. She rewarded them for their assignments, providing they were done properly. She helped them earn and budget money. She also taught them the importance of tithing. She taught them to be honest and treat others with respect. She taught the girls how to sew and cook meals (Roberta's college major was *home economics*). But what did I do with the children? Read on to the next paragraph.

My hobbies included science, sports, and gardening. I spent a lot of time with each of the children with their science fair projects. This became a highlight for each of our children. Not only did I help them how to construct various scientific models, but I also helped them learn and explain the scientific principles of their projects (present-day guidelines, regarding the performance of experiments on humans and other mammals, as the children did when they were young, is no longer permissible). I will provide an example of a project that each child performed: (1) created a water clock and explained how it works; (2) created a maze and had a mouse find its way through the maze. The mouse was timed to see how long it took going through the maze. Then the mouse was given alcohol to drink, and the experiment was repeated a second time. The object was to observe how alcohol affected the mouse's performance. (3) Another mouse experiment included using two mice that were placed on two diets and observing the results. One mouse was given a normal diet including all the essential vitamins. A second one was given a similar diet but was also fed raw eggs. The raw eggs caused a *biotin* deficiency. It demonstrated what can happen when the essential vitamin biotin is absent from a diet. (4) A fourth experiment was to have two persons eat two different types of breakfast cereals on two consecutive mornings, one person being a diabetic. The first morning included *Special K* and the second morning included a cereal that was commercially sweetened. Blood sugars were obtained from both subjects shortly after each cereal was eaten. The object was to observe which of the two cereals was the healthier for the diabetic patient.

Sports became a favorite pastime as well. I spent considerable time playing kickball and softball with all the children. As the two boys became old enough to play *little league baseball*, I became involved in coaching along with another coach. Our rules were slightly different from those of most coaches. We had a rule that each child would get to play a minimum of two innings, unless there was need for discipline. In such a situation, that child was not permitted to play that game. It was interesting, that one year, by holding fast to those roles, we were able to win the league. The concept of allowing all team members being allowed to play not only proved to be fair but also allowed every player to improve their skills and hence provided the team with more depth.

Learning how to garden was also a worthwhile adventure. It was exciting to observe a planted seed sprout and grow to give off its fruit. The downside of the gardening was also adventurous but not too exciting, because pulling or hoeing weeds was not fun. But not everything one does needs to be fun! To my surprise, all our children learned to appreciate the value of planting seeds and look forward to the time of harvest.

Because my free time was quite limited, I tried to give each of my children a special time with me, at least once a week. The principle was great but difficult to do because of the uncertainty of my after-work hours. Evening dinners were probably the best times for our family to be together. These were times when we would read interesting stories that contained spiritual lessons of life. It was also a time for entertainment. The children would frequently ask me to sing some humorous songs I had learned as a child. One of their favorite songs was about a donkey, because at the end of the song, I would imitate, singing, "Hee-Haw! Hee-Haw! Hee-Haw, Hee-Haw! Hee-Haw!" It was also a time when I would frequently use a common example to explain a scientific principle. An example would be "Do you know why your cap flies off your head when the wind is blowing?" Then I would explain Bernoulli's principle. The principle is this: Where the velocity is greatest, the pressure is least, and vice versa. Example of the cap: When the wind blows, the velocity of the wind is greater above the brim of the cap than it is below the brim. Below the brim of the cap, where the velocity is least, the pressure is greatest. Therefore, the wind does not blow the cap off one's head, but the increased pressure beneath the brim of the cap pushes the cap off the head. The children learned a lot of worthwhile things sitting around the Graber family table, from spiritual lessons to humorous entertainment, to practical lessons of science. Dr. Rodney Graber, my elder son, has written a few pages to be included in this book. He included some of the interesting times we all had around the dinner table.

It would not be appropriate to end this chapter about the family if I didn't share about my wife's death. She died prematurely from multiple strokes, resulting from a combination of atherosclerosis of the cranial arteries (hardening of the vessels of the brain) and Alzheimer's disease. She was a great individual and was most responsible for providing a wholesome environment for our children. After Roberta's death, I remarried a former high school classmate, Kathleen Ann (Klopfenstein) Cantrell. As was true about Roberta, Kathleen has been a loyal and loving companion and has brought happiness back into my life.

The following includes my tribute to my former wife, Roberta Mae Graber:

A TRIBUTE TO ROBERTA

Memories are the most pleasant thing,
So vivid tells its stories of past,
That in this trance I am wondering,
Will memories be memories that last?

Roberta, I remember how beautiful you appeared to me on that first day of our marriage. I remember the promises we made to each other—how I said I would take you to be my wedded wife—to love you and to cherish you—and to hold you as long as we both should live—through sickness and through health—till death doth we part.

Reflecting back on that first day together, I realized so little, the depth of your beauty. You have given us four beautiful and exceptional children and nine priceless grandchildren. You have taught them each how God's love reaches out to them and through them to be shared with others.

You have demonstrated to each of our children how to build lasting, wholesome family relationships. You were indeed a unique role model not only for us but also for many families to observe.

You allowed me to enjoy a life of interdependence with you. You allowed us to develop and express our love and gifts to many others. I never once was made to feel threatened about this interdependent relationship. Your love to me and to the family was contagious. You were like a butterfly, making no noticeable noise, fluttering about this great community of people, touching others with your smile and your warm caring heart. You left for all people of this community a legacy—a legacy of how God reached down to you and how you, in your own unique way, passed on his love to others.

I remember these last fifteen months of our life together. It became my turn to reach out to you, to fulfill my promise to care for you—"till death doth we part." I remember how difficult some of these moments were for us. I remember how we both asked God's forgiveness for each of us.

I remember when recently you said you were ready to be with Jesus, and we said it's okay with us. All these things I remember and many more!

Roberta, congratulations on a great and faithful life you lived—the precious moments you shared with our family and me and with this community. And congratulations upon your entry into Heaven. Your promise has been fulfilled. I hope to see you soon!

Your loving and faithful husband

Memorial picture of Roberta Graber, wife of Dr. Graber

CHAPTER 10

What Is a Calling?

You have read much of the story regarding my calling to become a physician. Reliving my own experience, I began to ask, "What reasons might others have had for choosing medicine as their career choice?" You will be interested in reading about twelve medical professionals who shared "Why I chose medicine as my career."

Defining a Calling

The *Merriam-Webster Collegiate Dictionary* defines *calling* as the following: (1) a strong inner impulse toward a particular course of action especially when accompanied by conviction of divine influence; and (2) a vocation or profession in which one customarily engages. From the quoted definition, I will include several life experiences from the Bible, of persons who received direct personal calls from the Creator. Then I will present stories from individuals who shared the reasons why they entered the medical profession. Most of these testimonials appear to fit the second part of the dictionary definition. All appear to have been touched by multiple environmental factors, including persons who had a special influence upon their lives, as well as other life experiences. One person heard a direct voice from God when attending a church camp retreat, stating, "I want you to become a doctor." Included in my experience was a professor who stated that she believed God had something else for me to do than to become a teacher.

Character Accounts from the Bible

The Bible relates stories of multiple characters whom God called to carry out specific work for his purpose. Examples of this included (1) Noah, whom God asked to have him build an ark (Genesis, chapter 6); (2) Moses, whom God asked to have him approach the king of Egypt to release *the Children of Israel* from captivity (Exodus 4 and 5); (3) Samuel, son of Hannah, heard his name called at night, three different times. When he went to the priest to ask what he wanted, he was told on the first two occasions to go back to sleep, for he had not called him. Following the third time that Samuel heard his name called, Eli, the priest, asked him to reply, "Speak, Lord, for your servant is listening" (1 Samuel 3). These three examples relate to a conviction of divine influence.

Character Accounts from Medical Professionals

From these interesting accountings, the reader should be able to take away from these personal stories several basic beliefs: (1) Environmental factors do play a major role for each individual in their decision-making process. (2) These environmental factors include early life experiences and special people who become their role models. (3) God does speak directly or through certain individuals regarding their life's calling. (4) It is by the *providence of God* (divine guidance) that we are given life's good experiences. (5) With all the environmental experiences and the divine advice we may be given, the choice is ours to accept or reject the path of life that becomes ours to travel. This brings me back to the introduction of this book. In it, I quoted Robert Frost and the poem he had written, *"The Road Not Taken."* The character who was traveling in that poetic story came to a fork in the road. Before continuing, he/she first studied the characteristics of the two paths, then made a choice as to which path should be traveled. And so it is with all of us; we become responsible in making a vocational decision of life that's best suited for us to travel. Like I had written about my path of life, I chose one less traveled by, and that has made all the difference. Next, enjoy the exciting environmental experiences from some of my medical colleagues and friends. Each was asked, "Why did you choose medicine as your vocation?"

Charles A. Bush, MD, FACC
Professor Emeritus, Cardiovascular Medicine
Ohio State University, Wexner Medical Center

My parents were both educators, and for as long as I can remember, education was emphasized to me. As a result, from a very early age, I wanted to excel at learning, and I took pride in having knowledge about anything and everything. I struggled a little with memorization but thrived on "figuring things out" and learning "how things worked." I loved to "fix" things and looked for the opportunities to take something apart and put it back together (hopefully in better working order). This allowed me to see the inner workings of things and things not apparent to the eye.

As I grew older and as realization hit that I would eventually need a job, I began to think about what I could do that would pique my interests. I had also identified "role models" for my life—each of my parents, my high school math teacher (I really liked math), and two uncles (both physicians). All five of these individuals were highly educated, and it seemed to me that they had immense knowledge about many (maybe all) things. They also interacted with many people and had an obvious (to me) influence on the lives of others. I developed a tremendous desire to emulate them all.

I briefly considered a career as a math teacher, but my father quickly quenched that thought by pointing out that it was a "dead-end street" in his opinion! Thus, I gravitated toward medicine as a career choice. What could be more exciting and stimulating than figuring out "how people worked"? Thus, from the middle of high school on, I was focused on learning about medicine and achieving a career in medicine.

This is really where the story starts, because little did I know about medicine: anatomy, physiology, biochemistry, and more. But I figured (correctly) that medicine was a field where I would never stop learning and gaining knowledge. In my opinion, there was no other field that would provide me with an opportunity to learn as medicine would.

Medical school proved to me how much there is to learn. It provided a tremendous challenge to me, and for the first time in my life, I struggled to learn. But it became rapidly apparent that medicine was where I could learn "the most." In addition, I was delighted to find out that I could also be a teacher and contribute to new knowledge in the field of medicine. It also became immediately obvious that I would have an influence on the lives of others. And when I found physiology (cardiology) was really the study of how people worked in a "makes sense" fashion, I became convinced that I had made the correct career choice.

So what started as a very selfish desire to learn about everything and become a "very smart person" morphed into a career where I could teach, contribute to new knowledge (research), care for patients, have a positive influence on the lives of others, *and* continue to learn.

Thus, becoming a physician led to far more than I ever expected when I initially made that choice. I have not for a second regretted that decision. My three-point formula for individual "success" and "career happiness" is as follows: (1) love what you do, (2) love those you work with, and (3) be intellectually stimulated in all that you do. Becoming a physician has allowed me to live those three points and influence the lives of others as well. Nothing could be better for me.

***

Robert H. Davis, MD, Ph.D., FCAP, FASCP
Chief of Pathology of Mary Rutan Hospital
Assistant Clinical Professor of Pathology
Ohio State University of Columbus, Ohio

This book details some of the many ways doctors choose to become physicians. Dr. Harry Graber was first a teacher and then heard the "calling" to become a physician.

We all have a varied path to medicine, whether it's a "calling" or for the love of science; individuals arrive at a destination and occupation from multiple different avenues. For me, it was the love of science. Chemistry always had my interest, and after a PhD degree in biochemistry, postdoc, and pharmacology, my path was changed due to a department chairman of pharmacology.

Professors and teachers have a profound effect on one's life. To nurture the ability of an individual is an art because everyone is an individual with different innate abilities. To activate these abilities is also a talent. In my case, it was a combination of professors and teachers, in addition to the love of science that created my career.

***

Evan W. Dixon, MD
Assistant Clinical Professor of Medicine
Division of Cardiology, Ohio State University

What Led Me to Become a Doctor

When I was a little boy, I was terrified by our family doctor. In the 1940s, the era of injectable antibiotics was flourishing. Seeing the doctor meant getting a painful shot, and I would resist with all my effort. It didn't matter that at age four I was bitten by a rabid dog. Fortunately, there was a rabies vaccine available, but it was a daily shot in the stomach wall for fourteen days with a large residual welt from the duck embryo vaccine. I remember the doctor trying to bribe me with a nickel, but I was having none of it.

I spent my childhood in Vinton County, Ohio. Our family operated a cattle farm with registered Herefords for breeding stock. There was no veterinarian in Vinton County, and I remember assisting my dad with castrations, hernia repairs, antibiotic injections, pinkeye treatment, and other sundry animal medical procedures. It was both scary and exciting.

My family attended a small Methodist church in our community. I eagerly looked forward to the summers when my friends and I attended a Methodist youth camp just outside Lancaster, Ohio. I don't remember much of the theology teachings, but I do remember eating tons of food, playing games, and noticing girls! As I recall, it was the summer after the eighth grade—my closest friend and I had had a spectacular week, and it was the last night of camp before returning home on Saturday. There was a beautiful outdoor chapel where evening vesper services were held. On that particular Friday night, the speaker challenged all of us to light a candle, find a place of solitude, and ask God to speak to us about what he wanted us to do with the rest of our lives. I remember sitting alone, watching the candle flame, and being intent on hearing a message from God. I was not disappointed. I didn't hear a voice, but I distinctly heard a voice in my head, saying, *I want you to become a doctor.* That was the last thing I would have thought about! Later, my friend told me he was to become a teacher. He is now a retired school superintendent, and I am still a practicing cardiologist. After that epiphany, I never questioned the decision. I don't know what I would have done with my life, because I never had a backup plan.

The memorable years of high school passed all too quickly—girls, studies, farm work, sports, and girls!

I was studious and managed to graduate as the valedictorian—in a class of nineteen! What I didn't know at the time was that my lack of preparation for college was almost insurmountable. I had one year of algebra; no physics, biology, chemistry, or formal writing classes. I finished all the credits available by the end of my junior year in high school, and that included Bookkeeping I and II and Typing I and II. I read a physics book and "dry labbed" the experiments; the principal gave me high school credit for physics without a teacher.

My family was not wealthy (but I didn't know that). I applied only to Ohio State University. I must have done well on the SAT tests, because I was offered a partial academic scholarship. I remember the high school principal coming to our house one evening, telling my parents that I would have lots of difficulty getting through Ohio State and little or no chance of attending medical school because of the huge holes in my educational background.

The principal was almost right. While many say their college years were the greatest, it was the most difficult period in my life. I was so far behind my peers that I was overwhelmed. I had to maintain a high GPR, work twenty hours a week, and average at least twenty-one hours of credit each quarter. I started drinking coffee and smoking cigarettes (long since abandoned) to stay awake. I abused my body with very little sleep, running on raw adrenaline and determination. I applied for early admission to medical school—again only at Ohio State—but was not accepted at the end of three years undergraduate. I was the first alternate for that year, but no one dropped out. My fourth year of college was fun. I took nonscience courses and already knew I would be entering the next year class.

Medical school was hard. I was ready to meet the challenge and was determined to be a top medical student. I can't say that God was occupying a major spot in my life during those college and medical school years—I was focused, perhaps driven, to excel. I was selected to remain at Ohio State for my postgraduate training. It was a golden time for medical training. The physician mentors had uncompromising standards of performance, and I received a tremendous gift of medical acumen and savvy from everyone around me. Those lessons learned in those days still serve me well at bedside or in the office.

When I finally decided to become a cardiologist, God, in his wisdom, provided a life-turning opportunity. I was set to leave for a job in Tennessee when a mutual friend of mine and this book's author suggested we talk about a cardiology partnering. That was the beginning of a long and wonderful relationship. I saw a colleague committed to his faith and reflecting it as a physician. We learned from each other. Although there were some bumps along the way, we knew that we were called to do this work of a physician. We have been both responsible and privileged. We have been in the intimate company of people at their best, at their worst, at their dying. We have come to sense the spiritual being and the spiritual yearnings of every person, regardless of their differences. We have learned not to judge but to extend comfort and assistance. Patients have taught us that death is not the enemy, but "living life in a void" is the worst disease possible.

I'm old now. The cost of practicing medicine has been high. I missed a lot. I missed family times, trips I would have liked to take, and hobbies I would like to have pursued. Despite the misses, I have been blessed beyond words. My spirit is calm. My heart is full. I know I did what I was supposed to do.

***

Carl V. Leier, MD, FACC
Professor Emeritus in the Emeritus Academy
Ohio State University

The Journey: Accounting for Career Choices

I retired about two years ago, after occupying the James W. Overstreet Chair (cardiovascular medicine) for thirty years, performing research in human cardiovascular disease for over forty years, and serving as the division director of cardiology at the Ohio State University Medical Center from 1986 to 1998. My colleague, Dr. Harry Graber, asked me to write this report on "How did you get here?" I know Harry well enough to recognize that this is not a casual query; I had to present facts and substance. Most everyone can recount their segments of history and careers, but rarely do we reflect on the whole journey; this interesting opportunity was presented to me by Dr. Graber.

I guess some of one's career course boils down to "being at the right place at the right time." But for me, "role models" have had a major impact on various points in my career.

I was born the last of ten children, seven surviving into the 1950s and beyond; a set of premature twins died shortly after birth in the late 1920s. In 1944, my second-eldest brother was killed when his B-17 bomber was shot down over Germany, seven days before I was born. We were raised on a family farm in South Central North Dakota, and there certainly was enough work for all of us. I attribute my work ethic and other personal characteristics to my first role models: my parents. My father taught me to persist until your job is done and also rendered to me a sense of organization and business. My mother's kindness and coolness under any situation did not escape my attention. All my brothers and sisters became successful local farmers-ranchers.

The education for my parents ended after the fourth grade. Except for my two eldest brothers and me, none of my siblings went to high school. I guess my father felt that the best job anyone could ever have in life was farming-ranching; the level of education needed and provided at that time (1950s) was simply to serve that specific purpose. How and why my parents allowed me to matriculate from the one-room country school (grades 1–8) to an all-boys boarding high school (St. John's Prep) more than three hundred miles from home in the middle of Minnesota remains a personal mystery to me. I assume my father saw that I had little aptitude for farming-ranching. Regretfully, I did not have enough sense to inquire about this matter while my parents were still alive.

And so at age thirteen, I was off to St. John's Prep. This was a pivotal point of my life. The four years there had an enormous impact on my future and my life choices. At ages thirteen through seventeen years and three hundred-plus miles from home, you learn how to survive, interact with others, and solve problems on your own while struggling through a rigorous curriculum. The prep school took this shy farm kid and molded me with the disposition, attitudes, and the various skills needed for my eventual career as an academic cardiologist at a Big Ten medical center. The Benedictine monks did not spare discipline, and they did not hesitate to apply whatever means it took to maintain such including eviction. My class started with about eighty boys and graduated forty-two seniors. I believe the only difference between a military prep school and St. John's is we did not wear uniforms and did not drill.

I was surrounded by brilliant young men from all over the country. Frankly, I worked my tail off to wind up ranked tenth in the class of forty-two. We were encouraged to play varsity sports and were always expected to perform our very best, similar to the expectations in scholastics. My role models at prep were my football and wrestling coaches, both firm in demeanor but kind. My football coach was also my college and career counselor; with my interest in the sciences, perhaps medicine, he suggested that I consider Creighton University in Omaha as the next step in my education. Knowing that he would not give me anything but the best advice, I never considered other options.

Starting in 1962, I attended Creighton University primarily as a science major and premedical student. Creighton is a fine university and consistently places high in the college rankings by US News and World Report. But Creighton Undergrad was a "breeze" compared to the scholastic intensity of prep; I guess St. John's did prepare me for college. I remember playing center fullback for the soccer team (then a club sport, which shortly thereafter became the varsity soccer team). Perhaps to improve my social skills (remember, St. John's was an all-boys prep school), I pledged and was inducted into Phi Kappa Psi, a social fraternity. I survived all that ("thrived" is a better descriptor) and maintained a grade point average such that after three years of undergraduate school, I was accepted without a bachelor degree into the Creighton University College of Medicine (1965).

Another key event occurred in 1963–1965 while I was an undergraduate. On evenings and on weekends, I washed glassware and cleaned equipment for a research laboratory nationally known for work in calcium metabolism, directed by Drs. Robert Heaney and Thomas Skillman. I got promoted to analyzing specimens for protocols, and in 1965, I wrote and submitted my first scientific abstract. To this day, I regard Dr. Heaney as the most intelligent person I ever met (and over the years, I've had the opportunity to rub elbows with some very smart people). Dr. Heaney went on to become the chief of medicine, then dean of the college and eventually, vice president of the medical complex. Dr. Skillman, another superb clinician and endocrinologist, went on to become the chief of endocrinology at the Ohio State University College of Medicine. I absolutely adored these two giants of medicine, whose talents as scientists and physicians were matched by their kindness and humility. They lit the flame for my enthusiasm and lasting interest in academic medicine and research.

I did find medical school at Creighton to be quite a challenge, requiring me to apply everything I learned and acquired at prep to meet this task head on. In 1969, I graduated from medical school at the top of the class; this written in all humility, simply to serve as a testimony to good training and education as a youth. I do recall a vignette which may be of interest: on the first day of medical school, I was standing at my locker, between two other classmates who had already earned their Ph.D. (or close to it) in biochemistry and biology. They were discussing their research, and frankly, I didn't understand anything they were talking about. I almost got "psyched out" and had to face the rhetorical question, "My goodness, what am I doing here?" While these two colleagues did not earn a place among my role models, they certainly inspired me to roll up my sleeves. I am forever grateful for the superb education I received at Creighton, for providing the role models of Drs. Heaney and Skillman, and for furnishing the training I needed to perform as an intern, resident, and doctor.

I met my future wife, a nursing student, during my junior year in medical school, another pivotal event in my life and career. We got married at the end of my internship. I wasn't aware of it at the time, but over forty-five years of marriage, I learned that she is the most sensible person I ever met. She had the patience to tolerate my medical career (which I regard as a very jealous mistress), raised our daughter and two sons with aplomb (complete and confident composure), and never complained about my underwhelming salary as a university research-cardiologist.

For house staff training, I considered Yale, University of Chicago, and Ohio State University. I selected Ohio State for three reasons: (1) its outstanding clinical training, which I believed had to form the foundation for whatever area in medicine I decided to pursue; (2) it was one of the few medical centers that required house staff to be on call at the hospital every other day-night, presumably to accumulate the most clinical experience possible. By then, Tom Skillman had moved from Creighton to Ohio State University as the chief of endocrinology (it was highly unlikely that Dr. Skillman would make a bad choice).

I started my internship (now referred to as year one of residency) at Ohio State in 1969. My medical knowledge and clinical experience grew exponentially that year. Being on call every other day-night and getting home quite late from the hospital on off-days basically meant that you lived at the hospital. I wouldn't trade that year for anything. I did not find the heavy caseload, grueling schedule, and lack of air conditioning (except for the Medical ICU) in hot-humid Columbus as significant distractions. But at the end of that year, I sheepishly decided that "I never wanted to see and care for a living, talking patient again"—perhaps a form of burnout.

I really enjoyed pathology as a medical student. And following my medical internship at Ohio State, I was accepted as a resident in pathology (where better can one find nonliving, nontalking patients) at St. Vincent Medical Center, Worcester, Massachusetts. I selected St. Vincent's because I took a one-month Medical ICU elective there as a medical student, and St. Vincent's was the professional home of Dr. Harold Jeghers (of the Peutz-Jeghers syndrome), a friend and colleague of Dr. Heaney (Creighton). My experience with clinical laboratory testing, dissecting surgical specimens, and performing necropsies was invaluable to me over the years as a clinician and researcher in human disease. My first paper was published that year in vascular surgery (Leier, C. V.; Dewan, C. J.; Anastasia, L. P. Fatal hemorrhage as a complication of neurofibromatosis. *Vascular Surgery* 6 (1972), 98–101). I eventually learned to appreciate live-patient interaction again and returned to Ohio State University (1971) to complete my medical residency and a cardiology fellowship.

Ohio State University was loaded with role models for me, far more than I can ever mention in this treatise. The residency director, Dr. Carl Metz, was a superb clinician and hematologist. Dr. James V. Warren, a world-renowned cardiovascular researcher, was then chief of medicine. When he asked me to serve as chief medical resident for the department in 1973–1974, I could not turn down that opportunity and privilege. In addition to gaining one more year of medical knowledge and experience, the chief residency under the guidance of Drs. Metz and Warren introduced me to the world and realities of administration, working with physicians and staff at all levels, and developing programs. During my medical residency, I became intrigued with the then–new diagnostic tools of cardiology (e.g., catheterization, echocardiography). Dr. Richard P. Lewis (then head of cardiology), another role model, likely influenced my decision to pursue cardiovascular medicine.

My cardiology fellowship was a nice mixture of clinical training and clinical research. The research initially involved human electrophysiology and heart failure, subsequently evolving into a total focus on heart failure. I was awarded a research fellowship with funding by the Central Ohio Heart Association, then a chapter of the American Heart Association.

Heart failure was particularly appealing to me because, at that time, it was essentially a wide-open area of investigation with available sources of extramural funding. As a junior faculty member, my first postdoctorate research fellow was Dr. Donald V. Unverferth, an energetic, innovative young investigator (whose academic background included serving as a three-year starting quarterback for Woody Hayes's Buckeyes in the mid-1960s). After Don joined the faculty at Ohio State, we divided our research efforts in heart failure along our lines of interest; Don pursued the human myocardial cell studies (via heart biopsies) and did our animal-based studies, and I performed the human hemodynamic and pharmacological studies. We became a very productive team, publishing more than ten papers per year in prestigious journals; attracting the best students, fellows, and postdoctorates to work with us; and accepting invitations worldwide to present our research. Interestingly, we never noticed that we were considerably underpaid as university cardiologists, and our wives never mentioned this shortcoming either. However, through the efforts of Drs. Joseph Ryan (senior staff cardiologist) and Richard Lewis, the Columbus Foundation, and the Seward Schooler Family Foundation, I was awarded the James W. Overstreet Chair in Cardiovascular Medicine in 1984, a chair I held until my retirement. What I regard as my "Camelot" period in clinical research slowed down in the late 1980s when Dr. Unverferth died of an astrocytoma, and I was asked to assume the directorship of cardiology at Ohio State. I lost a professional brother when Dr. Unverferth died. Drs. Philip Binkley, Garry Haas, and Randall Starling stepped in to carry on the research and clinical work in heart failure.

I reluctantly decided to accept the position of director of cardiology offered by E. L. Mazzaferri, MD, then chief of medicine—reluctant, because I regretted having to relinquish most of my research activities (which I regard as my primary aptitude). I was also aware of other candidates who were seeking directorship positions nationwide. Frankly, I decided I could do a better job than most of them. And importantly, I had a strong sense of loyalty and a deep collegial feeling for my colleagues at Ohio State. My "start-up package" as the new director was about $1.25; this check is still pending.

Most of the salaries for our cardiology faculty had to be generated from our clinical dollars, which, not surprisingly, may have distracted many faculty members from any type of research over the years (a problem common to most university clinical programs). Nevertheless, we held our own in this arena and strengthened several of our clinical programs such as electrophysiology, preventive-rehabilitative cardiology, echocardiography, and satellite clinics with more faculty and recruits from other universities (e.g., Duke, Cornell, St. Louis University).

After twelve years (1998), I stepped down as the director to serve out the remaining sixteen years of my faculty time at Ohio State as the Overstreet Professor, teacher (classroom and bedside), clinician (focus on heart failure and transplantation), and clinical researcher. In 2005, I received the Dr. Earl Metz Award for Excellence in Clinical Medicine from the Department of Medicine. I am now (2015) Professor Emeritus in the Emeritus Academy at The Ohio State University.

Comment from the author: Dr. Leier and I had several things in common: (1) We both attended a "one-room school." (2) We were both "farm boys." (3) He questioned whether his father might have thought he lacked the aptitude to be a farmer. My neighboring farmer thought I left for college was because I was too lazy to work. (4) We were in cardiology training together, dedicated to learn and serve humankind. But this was where the commonality ended. Dr. Leier already exhibited the intellect and the accumulative clinical experience like that of a professor, while I presented as a typical, Level 1 cardiology fellow, eager to learn the basics of cardiology.

**

Glen E. Miller, MD, FACP
Internal Medicine

The Making of a Doctor

I grew up in a family of nine children during the Great Depression. For our family to survive the hard times, we had to stick together. It was assumed that the needs of the family came before any individual needs. Deferring to one another was necessary and a way of life. Beginning age thirteen, each summer I worked for my uncle, helping make hay or do other farm work. My uncle wanted no idle hands. One time, during a break from making hay, he told me, "While you're resting, move that pile of bricks to the back of the barn." At the end of the week, I turned over the money I earned to my father. I was allowed to keep one-eighth of the money; the rest went to sustain the family. I never questioned the system. It was the way things were done.

At the age of twelve, I read a book that changed my life. I have no idea where the book *Dr. York, Hill Doctor* came from or how it came into my possession. I read the entire book practically in one sitting. The next day I picked up the book and read it a second time. Young Dr. York had left the comforts and well-heeled confines of a large city to go to the hills of Eastern Kentucky to provide medical care to a community where none existed. After reading that book, I quietly decided I wanted to be like Dr. York. (I have looked for that book since, without success.)

At first I told no one of my aspirations to become a doctor, not even my parents. I knew that my cousins would have looked at me with derision for harboring such a ridiculous notion. Later, at a family gathering, my mother was asked which one of her boys was going to be a doctor. She pointed to me and said, "He *thinks* he is." I understood. It was presumptuous for a farm boy, raised during the Great Depression, to think of (much less verbalize) such a lofty goal. In that era, doctors were revered with a level of respect that made them near-mythical beings.

I was drafted during the Korean War, and following my Mennonite pacifist upbringing, I registered as a conscientious objector. As an alternative to military service, I worked in a mental hospital as a ward orderly. My supervisors, at my request, assigned me to night duty, which freed me to go to classes at Kent State University. I eventually graduated from Goshen College. By taking summer courses, I completed the premedical studies in three years. It was a glorious day when I was accepted at Western Reserve School of Medicine in Cleveland in 1957.

Medical school was as rigorous as expected. Marilyn Oswald and I had married before medical school and, during those four years, had three children. There were added pressures because we never had money (I use "we" in this context because it is difficult to use the singular after decades of married life). Between babies, Marilyn worked as a part-time nurse. The last two years, I "externed" as a medical student in a Good Samaritan Hospital that provided room and board and $50 per month. Thus we were able to control our debt level.

Following graduation and one year of internship, we volunteered to go for two years to Haiti to work in a small hospital. Part of my motivation for going to Haiti was because I was keenly aware of those of my generation who had gone to Korea and fought. Some had died there. Serving Haiti was an attempt to do my part in a small way. In retrospect, this seems to be the first installment on living out my goal as a twelve-year-old to go into medicine to serve poor people.

I found that service was pleasure. The two years in Haiti put us in touch with some of the poorest people in the world. We saw individuals struggle with the things we take for granted like food, clothes, and a roof over our heads. And most Haitians did this with grace. We also got a picture of our own country from the viewpoint of Haitians, with its wealth and emphasis on consumerism and materialism. We were determined to be known for who we are, not what we own.

After a year of postgraduate training in family practice, it was time to find a place to settle in and raise our four children. Our country home near Bellefontaine, Ohio, was an ideal setting for these purposes.

Ten years after we were married, I was ready to start medical practice. Up to that point, we had lived in thirteen places in ten years. Moving had become a way of life. After six months, our small children wondered when we were going to move again. Our combined income for the first ten years of our marriage was slightly over $2,000 per year.

I became a founding member of a group medical practice that eventually grew to eleven members. Dr. Harry Graber became one of my medical partners in 1966. I was in family practice from 1965 to 1971. Four of those years I served as the county health commissioner. From 1971 to 1973, I was in internal medicine residency training and became certified in internal medicine.

The following years were filled with office and consultative practice. Harry Graber and I, along with others, worked hard, persistently to improve the quality of care in our local hospital. We eventually achieved recognition as one of the top small hospitals in the state of Ohio. In 1990, I left my position as medical director of the hospital to go to India where Marilyn and I served Mennonite Central Committee for seven years.

Now in my eighth decade and looking back, I see a pattern of one decision leading to another. I ask myself, *What is the common thread that runs through a life that became involved in widely varied activities, traveling to more than forty countries and living overseas for more than eleven years in five countries?* What I do know is that my childhood formation in growing up in a big family under my mother's gentle and compassionate tutelage, my father's core principles of honesty and integrity, and my identity within a strong Mennonite community have all contributed immeasurably.

Now at age eighty-two, I continue to be engaged with my family—except for taking a nap whenever they play cards—and with an ever-expanding community. I will resist becoming a bystander as long as I have my strength and my mental faculties.

Throughout my life I was fascinated by the stories of people—stories from farmers in Ohio to farmers in India, the life-changing story of a childhood accident, the story of survival through the holocaust in Cambodia, or the triumph over oppression by a group of Indian women through their collective efforts. I was seldom at a loss for words when meeting a stranger or old acquaintance alike because I always knew there was something to learn from them. I don't recall anyone I considered boring—well, maybe a few after twenty minutes of conversation. So even in the ninth decade of life, I avidly listen to stories with a view to learn how it helps me understand life. I take seriously what I hear and test it to see how it adds to or fits with what I believe to be true. In listening to others' stories, I have lost the need to judge; conversely, I am grateful that the other person confides in me.

There were a number of critical decision points in our lives (mine and Marilyn's), where had we taken the other fork in the road, the destination would have been vastly different. As I look back, it is not entirely clear how we made those decisions. What is clear is that we were influenced in those decisions by our Anabaptist heritage, a strong community, and the idea that some of our energies needed to be spent in serving others. We tried to take seriously the words of Jesus on how to live and relate. We preferred hospitality and gentleness to coercion and confrontation. The thread that seems to run through our varied experiences is the desire to serve. In serving, we were in turn served by so many along the way. For that, I am grateful.

Along the way, I found purpose, even joy, in the feeling that I was contributing to a better life for those with whom I came in contact. In some measure, I felt that I had achieved my boyhood dream of service to those in need. The words of the Nobel Prize–winning Indian poet Rabindranath Tagore, capture my feelings:

> *I slept and dreamed that life was pleasure,*
> *I woke and saw that life was service,*
> *I served and found that service was pleasure.*

***

Vincent Petno, MD, FACC
Cardiologist

All-American Football Athlete Chooses Medicine as His Calling

My story begins in an ethnic Italian community in a small coal mining town south of Pittsburgh, Pennsylvania, called Uniontown. My mother was a seamstress who only finished the eighth grade of school. My father was a coal miner and the only one to complete high school in his family. My only sibling was an elder brother.

Education was very important to my parents, and they worked very hard "so our sons could go to college." They had hoped that one of us would become a doctor. My brother graduated from West Virginia University as a geologist.

In high school, I was an above-average student but did not work up to my potential academically. I was more interested in sports, which I participated in year round. My senior year, because of football, I received an appointment to the U.S. Naval Academy. But I did not meet the English pretest standard for entrance. I subsequently went to the Citadel, a military school in South Carolina, to play football on a scholarship after my freshman year.

Starting college, I had no real direction concerning a life's career. My mother had always said, "You are going to be a doctor!" Based on her desire and insistence, I began a premed curriculum at the Citadel and although very difficult, I realized the medical field was maybe a good match for me.

Because of God-given talents, I had a successful college football career and had many postseason accolades and was drafted by the Oakland Raiders.

Immediately after graduating from college, I married a young lady from my high school, who was a nurse. Although we occasionally went to church, God was really not a part of our lives in any practical way.

I applied to all the medical schools in my home state of Pennsylvania but did not gain entrance mainly because I had gone out of state for undergraduate study. Competition for medical school slots was very competitive and mainly obtained by students from Pennsylvania who did undergraduate study in that state.

It appeared that I was not going to be a physician and was going to initially be on the Oakland Raider football team. I had signed a contract with that team that stated I would play if I did not get into medical school. However, before giving up the quest to become a physician, I applied to the

Medical College of South Carolina, which happened to be in Charleston, South Carolina, where I went to college at the Citadel.

In retrospect, I strongly believe that God was working in my life, and his plan was for me to become a physician. Although I had the academic credentials and MCAT score needed for admission, I was not successful in my home state. To my surprise, I was accepted to medical school in South Carolina and believe my football career had something to do with my being chosen.

Although the difficulty of being newly married and beginning medical school, it became immediately apparent to me that this vocation was a great match for me. I loved what I was learning, as well as the challenge.

My freshman year, I met Peter Gazes, MD, who was a cardiologist who was one of our professors. We had opportunity to be with him on rounds, and I was amazed at his ability to examine the cardiovascular system at the bedside and make diagnoses and decisions with very few aids. I believe it was my freshman year I decided, "I wanted to become a cardiologist like Dr. Gazes."

I was fortunate my senior year to spend a preceptorship with Dr. Gazes, which cemented my desire to become a clinical cardiologist. After my internship, time in the USAF, and medical residency, I was fortunate to train at the Cleveland Clinic and become a clinical cardiologist in 1975. During my training, I was involved in Bible studies. In 1974, God gave me the faith to believe that Jesus Christ died for my sins and based on that fact he saved me and I was born again.

I practiced as a cardiologist for twenty-two years. The last thirteen years were as a partner with Cardiology Associates of Bellefontaine, Ohio. Dr. Harry Graber, one of the partners, had been chief resident and mentor when I was an intern in Akron, Ohio. I retired from medicine in 1997.

***

By permission, I am including this next person's story, who by request is not named. This physician tells an early life story that many of us can relate to. We are all products of unique environmental experiences. Some of these may deter us temporarily from a goal that is providentially designed for us. While some early experiences temporarily behave as hindrances, later in life, they serve as tools to help others. This physician is one of the most loved and respected persons I know. In my mind, he made the right decision. Medicine became his unique *tool* to reach out to people who were in need. The following is his story.

No member of my father's or my mother's family was involved in the fields of medicine or nursing in any way. From childhood, I was always interested in airplanes and dreamed of someday being a professional pilot. In the late 1940s and early 1950s, the overwhelming percentage of airline pilots were former military pilots, and I realized that I would never succeed as a pilot applicant in the air force because of my less-than-perfect vision, and I gave up hopes of a career in aviation.

I attended a Jesuit high school where the emphasis was firmly placed on a liberal education. My teachers were all members of the Jesuit order—priests and scholastics; in the Jesuits, ordination usually occurs only after thirteen to fifteen years of study involving multiple under graduate and graduate degrees and several years of teaching at the high school and/or university level. I was very much impressed by my teachers who lived lives devoted to study, scholarship, teaching, and "good works."

I went off to college with no good idea of what to do with my opportunities and my life; my limited goal was to get as liberal an education as possible. By the end of my second year, my mother was getting quite concerned that I was just drifting along without any clear plan or goal in life and asked me from time to time if I had any career plans. I knew that I didn't want to be a lawyer like my father, and as best as I could tell, I was not likely to succeed in a business career. Although aptitude tests, which my classmates and I took in the week before starting my freshman year in college, had indicated that I was much better suited for engineering than for the liberal arts, I couldn't see myself succeeding as an engineer or doing anything with my hands.

At this point, there were two principal options in my mind: a career in the church or in medicine. Raised in the Episcopal Church, I had always been a faithful attendee at Sunday school and later at Sunday early services. However, I never seriously considered myself an appropriate candidate for a career in the church.

This left medicine as the last reasonable option. I have been very fortunate in my personal health and, when young, was exposed only to outpatient ENT care for recurrent sinus problems and for eye evaluations for restoration of visual acuity. Our ENT physician was a very competent and highly regarded surgeon with very pleasant manners. My parents had several physicians who were their friends and always spoke favorably of them. I decided to attempt a career in medicine even though I had already completed two years of college and had not taken any premedical science courses (I had doubts whether I could handle the rigorous required chemistry and biology courses). Thus, I enrolled in an eight-week beginning chemistry course in July between my second and third years of college. In third year, I took a beginning course in biology plus chemical qualitative analysis in the first semester. The only course available for me to meet the requirement for organic chemistry was a class intended for the chemical engineering majors, which started in the beginning of the second semester of third year and finished at the end of the first semester of fourth year. I was very lucky in this because I was able to take my organic chemistry in a small group (ten or twelve) who were supposedly socially deprived "geeks" or "grinds," who turned out to be wonderful friends. I purposely avoided the standard organic chemistry class that consisted of 150–200 intensely competitive premedical students. The biology courses I took held no interest for me.

When the time came in the senior year for me to apply to medical school, I applied to Harvard, Columbia, Johns Hopkins, Creighton, and Nebraska on the advice of a family friend who at the time was a cardiovascular surgery fellow at Columbia Presbyterian Medical Center. The dean of admissions at Columbia came to the Yale campus to interview applicants; Johns Hopkins had a local physician interview applicants. For my application to Harvard, I had to miss most of my classes on a Wednesday, drive through heavy traffic to Boston, find parking, locate a basement office in the dental school, and be interviewed by a member of the dental school faculty. The interviewer's main focus was to know why I wanted to be a doctor and what made me think I had the needed qualifications. Needless to say, I felt very fatigued and stressed by the trip (no lunch, late afternoon interview). The interview was shortened considerably (I think) by admitting that I had no good answer as to why I wanted to be a doctor. I left feeling that I had botched up everything and made a fool of myself. As I drove back to New Haven, the realization came to me that what I would really like to do would be to teach Latin and Greek in a private secondary school as one of my friends was doing at Pomfret School. Although I did enjoy my chemistry courses, I had no interest in biology, and even the courses in my English major were becoming tedious. With my decision to pursue a career in teaching Latin and Greek and abandon all plans for medicine, my spirits soared, and for the first time in days, I felt a great surge of energy and enthusiasm. I returned to our dormitory room and was greeted by my roommate. He had a large can of beer in one hand and a fat unopened envelope in the other hand. With obvious delight, he handed me the unopened envelope, assuring me that a fat envelope from Columbia P and S must surely mean I was accepted into the next entering class. My roommate and my brother, whose quarters were adjacent, were delighted and in a party mood. I could not bring myself to tell them that I had decided that a career in medicine was not for me, nor did I tell my parents. With a heavy heart, I made the decision that I had started down the road to being a physician and that whether I liked it or not simply didn't matter. I thought to myself, I needed to shut up, not complain, and do the work as best I could, accepting whatever came. After all, this is what my Jesuit teachers had to commit to—their vows of poverty, chastity, obedience, and a life devoted to study and teaching. As the Jesuits told me, I needed to lead a "life for others."

For quite some time, I have had the belief that one learns to be a good caregiver at home, long before one enters medical school to master the basic knowledge and technical expertise to take on the responsibilities of the care of patients. I think it is very difficult, if possible at all, to teach medical students, or nurses for that matter, to be sensitive, interested, respectful, and compassionate caregivers. In retrospect, I suspect that I went into and remained in the practice of medicine because it provided the best match for the character traits which my parents, especially my mother, wished me to have.

One day in the operating room many years ago, I remember hearing the late heart surgeon, Dr. James Kilman, say, "I would rather be lucky than smart." I have been lucky as illustrated by my choice of a career in medicine.

Comment from the author: By all who know this physician, he cared for his patients with much kindness and servitude. He followed the Jesuit's advice very well. He lived his life for others, and medicine became the *vehicle* to accomplish that goal.

***

Stephen Schaal, MD, FACC
Professor of Medicine, Division of Cardiology
Emeritus Status, Ohio State University

Reflections in Becoming a Physician

From about the sixth grade on, I was thinking about medicine—primarily motivated by books read and observations of one of my most revered individuals—my best friend's father who was a physician.

Part of my family and I went to the Christian Science Church; this presented a major barricade toward adopting medicine as a career until I talked with one of the Christian Science leaders after my first year at Ohio Wesleyan University. It was then that I switched from engineering to the "premed" track. I loved the sciences—particularly organic chemistry and physiology—subjects where I could see the links between health and disease. My years at Ohio Wesleyan, in addition to being most enjoyable, were visionary for me as I took as many English courses as I could as well as history courses. The liberal arts background suited me well and provided a framework for understanding social issues and being sensitized to individual and patient needs.

I entered medicine at the Ohio State College of Medicine (1960) and enjoyed everything right from the onset. I read the cardiac physiology text during the summer months after my first year and was hooked on cardiology. After my second year, I did cardiology research (ECG study) and knew then that I would pursue an academic career in cardiology. I was exposed to some excellent physicians in medical school (and a cardiology veterinarian) who provided ample insights toward being a good scientist and humanistic physician.

I did my internship, residency, and cardiology fellowship at Duke University. Again, some great clinicians and researchers. I received an intense but most enjoyable training while starting a research career in cardiac electrophysiology. After a couple of years doing cardiac research in the air force at Wright Patterson AFB in Dayton, Ohio, I was recruited to the Ohio State Medical Center by Drs. Arnold Weissler and James Warren. I started OSU's first cardiac exercise evaluation and cardiac rehabilitation programs since such did not exist at OSU. I then embarked on human electrophysiology studies since I had been continuing my basic animal electrophysiology research.

I've had some great associates over the years of my teaching, clinical care and research endeavors at OSU—particularly the cardiology division. I've particularly enjoyed the teaching and interaction with the many outstanding cardiology fellows who have trained with us. I also enjoyed the administrative responsibilities and leadership roles with the American Heart Association, the American College of Cardiology, the OSU Hospital Aboard, chairing the OSU Ethics Committee, etc. Medicine is in good hands and moving forward with some very dedicated physicians and leaders.

***

Grant Varian, MD, Internal Medicine
Medical Director of Mary Rutan Hospital

Early Experiences That Guided Me into Medicine

In my childhood and youth, I lived, played and worked on our family farm, Varian Orchards. We lived a half-mile back off the road in the middle of the farm and two and a half miles from East Canton, Ohio. I don't know exactly when I became interested in science, but I don't believe I was unique. I learned about facts of nature and became curious. I had a small "laboratory" in our basement where I worked with my chemistry set (a Gilbert). I played around with radios and stereos, adding speakers, changing the antennas. I recall constructing a crystal set. I had the most fun one summer in the eighth or ninth grade when my father and his good friend's father hired our high school chemistry teacher to tutor us in the science of rocketry. We had a ball! I accumulated equipment for my lab, such as beakers, flasks, clamp stands, test tubes. In school, as I progressed through my primary and secondary years, I seemed to have an aptitude and certainly an interest in all the sciences.

Throughout most of those years, I always expected that I would follow my father's footsteps into pomology (science and practice of growing fruit) and eventually live on and operate our orchard. By the time I became a teen, I already had learned a lot about the fruit-growing business and routine responsibilities around the farm. However, my plans to grow and sell apples, peaches, and cherries for a living came to an end, one hot July afternoon in my eleventh grade of school. I was in one of our orchards on the side of a hill with the assignment to spot-pick (choosing only the apples that were ready) the Lodi, an early apple excellent for cooking. The trees were standard stock and mature, so they were big, requiring a long ladder. The work was tedious and tough. As I toiled away, I realized something very important. I did not want to earn my living in life, working as hard as my father did. As much as I loved the farm, I knew at that moment that my future was not there.

Over the next year, I decided that I wanted a career in science. I was interested in chemistry and finally concluded that my goal would be an educational career in biochemistry, as a bench scientist. Even by then, I had not really given medicine much consideration. My exposure to the profession was fairly limited. I respected and appreciated our family physician, whose office was in East Canton. He and his family, who were members of our church, were very involved in our community and were incredibly generous. However, I don't recall by my late high school years about any serious thoughts in becoming a physician. That would change later on.

It was late in my second year at Ohio State when I decided that my goal should be a career in medicine. My major study until then had been, as planned, biochemistry in the College of Agriculture. At that time in college, I was very active in extracurricular activities on campus and was thoroughly enjoying them. Eventually, I realized that I would be happier in my life's work if I was working with and around people to a greater extent than promised to be the case in a lab. I adjusted my course selection to meet the prerequisites for application to medical school.

I began my studies at the College of Medicine at Ohio State University in July 1967. The basic science years were about as anticipated. Most of the coursework was lecture and test with the exception of the practical labs. Obviously, these courses were necessary and served me well as my experience expanded, but the highlight for me of those early years was our work with physical diagnosis. We were blessed to have superb medical instructors: Dr. Prior (pulmonology), Dr. Sauders (ENT), Dr. Beman (GI), and especially Dr. Wooley (cardiology). Dr. Wooley was not only an outstanding teacher of physical diagnosis of the cardiovascular system, but he also had high expectations of how we appeared and conducted ourselves as students. One day, on clinical teaching rounds, I made a mistake of leaning back against the doorframe during a case discussion in the hall. Dr. Wooley noticed my lowering of the guard and pounced immediately. He interrupted the case discussion and "dressed me down" in no uncertain terms about professional appearance and behavior, and I was not meeting those standards on that occasion. Oh, and I believe my lab coat was unbuttoned as well. Of course I was embarrassed, but it was a lesson learned.

Our clinical years were intense. The days were long and the learning was constant. Of course, there were no limitations on how long we would be in the hospital. One stayed until the work was done. We had a superb clinical experience, which of course included the full complement of problem assessment. We also had excellent hands-on experiences, performing some of the basic laboratory testing, such as analyzing urine specimens, blood smears, stool guaiac, and gram stains. The different medical specialty rotations provided interesting learning experiences. Of all the specialty rotations, I appreciated obstetrics the least. The process of "getting those little babies out and started up" scared the "dickens out of me"!

Early in my fourth year of medical school, I began researching residencies and interviewing where I wanted to go for my postmedical education. It was always my intention to practice family medicine, but family medicine residencies were just beginning to appear. I believe there were only about five programs nationwide at that time (1970). I interviewed at Rochester, New York; York, Pennsylvania; and Newport Beach, California. There were no programs in Ohio. Of the three, I elected the York program, which seemed to be the most established. I knew I was in trouble, though, when they asked me during the interview if I intended to practice in the York region or at least in Pennsylvania. Since I had always intended to practice somewhere in Ohio, I truthfully answered no. They responded that practice location intention would be considered as they ranked for the match. Since I had concluded that I would not rank the other programs that I had visited, I began to work on my plan B. Dr. Michael Anthony, the director of postgraduate training at Mount Carmel Medical Center in Columbus, told me that they were in the process of developing a family medicine residency and that it would be accredited in time for me to become board eligible. So in the match, I ranked York first and Mount Carmel second. I matched with Mount Carmel.

It was during my internship training at Mount Carmel that it became clear to me what specialty of medicine got my attraction. My first rotation was pediatrics and Children's Hospital of Columbus. My second rotation was internal medicine. It wasn't long into that assignment that "I became hooked"! I completed my internal medicine training and became certified in June 1974. Meanwhile I was selected to serve as chief resident of internal medicine. It wasn't long into the assignment that I was contacted by Dr. Glen Miller, who had also trained at Mount Carmel Medical Center and was now at Mary Rutan Hospital at Bellefontaine, Ohio. He was the sole specialist in internal medicine at that hospital (Dr. Harry Graber had just left to begin his cardiology training at Ohio State University) and was overwhelmed with work. Dr. Miller appealed to me to leave my chief medicine assignment to join him at Oakhill Medical Associates to begin practice with him. I accepted his appeal and moved to Bellefontaine, Ohio, with my family. We were very busy. Upon Dr. Graber's return, following his cardiology training, he elected to split away from Oakhill Medical Associates (OMA), to begin solo practice in cardiology. Soon after, we also left OMA where we moved into a new building facility (1980). It included the specialties of internal medicine, cardiology, and general surgery.

In 1985, my wife, Martha (Marty) was diagnosed with breast cancer. She died in September of 1987. Glen and the cardiologists (Dr. Graber and Dr. Dixon) provided coverage for me while I was away about half of the time in 1987 during my wife's terminal illness.

Dr. Miller and I were partners for nearly fourteen years when he made a career change and left practice in 1988. After his departure, three different internal medicine specialists became short-term partners with me, one leaving to return to Indiana University, to enter into academic medicine, another leaving to move to Alaska, and a third partner left to begin her family. A fourth internist, Dr. Winfred Stoltzfus, joined me in 1993. Because of financial difficulties, he and I became employed by Mary

Rutan Hospital. From 2002 on, I have been serving as medical director of the hospital. In addition, I provided part-time care for indigent patients, through the outpatient clinic of the hospital until the end of 2014.

Comment from the author: In this physician's experience, the things that stand out include early childhood experiences as arranged by his father, then later on, experiences from persons outside the home environment, such as mentors in college, then medical school and postgraduate training. As it was with me, this physician experienced the death of a spouse, but in his case, when she was quite young. As painful as that and other experiences are, they become instrumental in caring for certain other patients. Through it all, Dr. Varian continues to serve his medical community with much dedication and purpose.

***

Testimonials from Persons Who Received Medical Experiences During High School

Back in the 1980s and early 1990s, a summer employment program was set up for high school students who were thinking about future adventures in health care. Those who inquired about summer employment were interviewed by me. If I felt there was keen interest in pursuing a vocation in the healthcare industry, they would be considered for summer employment on a first-come basis. (The program could accommodate up to two persons per summer.) Over a period of time, about ten to twelve students had participated in the program. Four in this group responded to my invitation, requesting "Why did you choose medicine as your vocation?" You will enjoy their responses.

***

Albert Massaquoi, Physician's Assistant

***

Why I Became Interested in Health Care

Twenty-one years ago, I arrived in the United States from West Africa in search of a better opportunity, better career, and a better life. As a young man, I realized that the opportunities ahead of me in an unknown country were better than the struggles I have come to know for over seventeen years in my war-torn country of Sierra Leone where the future of young men was without promise. Through the generosity of a well-known American cardiologist, Harry Graber, MD, I was offered an opportunity to further my education in the United States of America.

Three months prior to meeting Dr. Graber, I was approached by a family acquaintance about considering a summer job serving aboard the maritime ship called the *Anastasis,* which will soon dock in the ports of Freetown to provide medical services to the needy. "You will be paid a lot of money for your services," he said. "How much?" I asked in excitement. "Less than five dollars per day, and you will get a free meal while on duty."

Well, this was certainly not my idea of a lucrative summer job especially with the type of compensation that was being offered, so I decided to volunteer instead. Each morning we would divide ourselves into teams— dental and medical teams, respectively. As a young African boy, I knew that I would serve humanity one day in some capacity when I became of age and the medical profession was one of the best ways that I could accomplish this dream if my faith did not waver in the process.

Being part of the medical team was certainly a great opportunity for me to learn firsthand what a typical day is like in the life of the physician. The medical team was responsible for establishing tents as makeshift clinics in remote parts of Sierra Leone. They would spend eight to ten hours a day providing medical care to the villagers. This opportunity gave me the ability to translate English into Creole and Mende so that the tribespeople can understand what they were being told by these English-speaking healthcare providers. In my capacity as a translator, I also learned pharmacy technician skills and assisted in minor surgical procedures without any formal medical training. Observing doctors and nurses perform their duties with grace and selflessness quickly captivated my mind and wished I was trained to do the same. One week later, I was approached by my new friend Dr. Graber asking if I would consider pursuing a career in health care either in the United States or in any other country that I felt comfortable. I decided that America would be that place.

On July 17, 1994, I arrived in the United States to start a future that has been afforded me by a generous Christian doctor and his wife and entire family. The Graber family was now my new family, and I quickly became acclimated to their simple and humble lifestyle. Speaking with friends of Dr. Graber, after Sunday worship service, I quickly learned that most of their children were either in medical school or pursuing academic degrees in chemistry, biology, or other related disciplines. This was now my new reality compared to the rebel war that devoured most of my childhood friends. My dream of studying medicine was finally within reach.

Great things have happened in my life since I arrived in my new home twenty-one years ago, some of which cannot be chronologically documented in this account, but I hope to do so someday. Today, through the financial support of the Graber family, I can confidently say that I have accomplished all the goals that were set before me and in some cases more than I expected. I have been blessed with the opportunity to pursue masters and doctoral degrees in some of the finest universities the world has ever known, and my desire to serve the human populace has never been stronger than it is today. For the past nine years, I have had the privilege of practicing medicine in the disciplines of gastroenterology and emergency medicine. A dream of becoming a medical practitioner that seemed so distant at some point in my life is a reality today. Opportunities are given, but success in life is earned by having a "can do" attitude and using the gifts that God has given every one of us to serve others. In the Bible, we are reminded in Jeremiah 29:11-13 that God has a plan of hope and an expected future for our lives if we diligently seek him with all our heart. I have been blessed beyond measure to stretch God's healing hands to the sick through the gifts he has entrusted into my care. America, a place that I now call home for over twenty years, is worth defending from the hands of the enemy. As a lieutenant in the United States Armed Forces, I have promised to care and defend its citizens from war and disease. America and its people have provided me with hope, liberty, and the pursuit of my own personal happiness without asking much in return. It is now my opportunity to give in kind my services and skills which have been bestowed upon me by God Almighty.

Comment from the author of this book: Albert Massaquoi has been a real blessing to us. He is now married to a beautiful wife, Elizabeth, formerly from the Congo. They are currently living in Texas. He is finishing his doctorate degree at Nova Southeastern University, a privilege afforded him from where he is currently employed, where he will be working in medical research.

***

Matthew Ray Steiner, MD, Emergency Medicine

Why I Wanted To Be a Physician

When I think back as to when I made a decision to become a doctor, it often makes me appreciate the examples that I had to follow before me. Being adopted and coming here from Vietnam when I was eight years old,

I consider myself to be one of the luckiest persons on earth. I was adopted by a wonderful Christian family who lived in West Liberty, Ohio. West Liberty is a small rural town with a tight-knit community. My adoptive family consisted of my father, Dr. James Steiner, along with my mother, Mary Steiner. I had three brothers, Dan, Doug, and Jeff.

One of the main reasons that I wanted to become a physician was what I witnessed by the life of my adoptive father. He was a family practice–trained physician. From my observations, he was well trained in many specialties, particularly in surgery and OB-GYN. This would serve him well during his many years as a missionary doctor. I can remember him telling me about many surgeries, including appendectomies, that he did during his years on the mission field. I also remember everyone in the community telling me that my father practically delivered "almost everyone" in the town. I do remember one stormy night in the blizzard of 1978—some called this the "storm of the century." The roads were impassable because of several feet of snow, with gusts of wind surpassing 50 mph. My dad got a call informing him that one of his patients was going into labor. There was no way for him to get to the hospital by car. A snowmobile had to come out to our house, and he did manage to arrive to the hospital in time for the delivery. My father, as I stated before, was a medical missionary doctor. He served in a leprosy camp in Vietnam for two years. Then he served in Thailand for one year before serving two or three years in Africa. He then returned to the United States to begin his family practice in West Liberty, Ohio. When I arrived to the United States in 1975, he served one year with the Indian Health Service in Crown Point, New Mexico. I was fortunate to be with our family during this time and was able to share in the experience living on a Navajo Indian Reservation.

One of the proudest things that I always say is that all the brothers were born in different countries. Dan, the eldest, was born in the United States before leaving on their first missionary trip. Doug was born in Vietnam. Jeff was born in Thailand, and I was born in Laos. I have always admired my father, especially his dedication and caring spirit. He always thought of how he could serve others and made their lives a little easier. What made him stand apart was that he showed by example of how you can do this. I was always impressed with how he sacrificed his comfortable life in the United States. Instead of having a "doctor's income" and living in a nice house with nice things, he chose to have his entire family living in a third-world country. As my mom has told me, those were exciting days. I can't imagine the faith that he had, as he faced many situations that he was not trained for. He not only dealt with difficult medical situations during his residency program but also had to face many challenges, living in the third world.

I have always admired what a difference my dad made in another person's life. This was also true of another doctor whom I admired in our community. Dr. Harry Graber was that other person who made a difference in everyone's life. I was a good friend to Dr. Graber's son, Rodney. I was often in their home to witness how Dr. Graber interacted not only with his family but also with friends of the community. The Grabers have always made me feel like a part of their family. This was even more pronounced after the sudden accidental death of my adoptive father. I will always be thankful to Dr. Graber for taking the lead in providing a role model after my father's death. He was always available to talk and give me great advice on many things.

As you can see, I have two physicians whom I truly respected and looked up to for guidance. It is interesting that my adoptive father never pushed me to go into medicine. I was a good student and graduated as valedictorian in my class. I think my father knew that I was capable of going through the hard road of medical school and residency to become a doctor. I really appreciate that he did not force me to follow in his footsteps, even though I think he would have been very happy with that decision. As I went to college, I was unsure whether I wanted to become a doctor. I studied premedical courses at Goshen College and majored in biology. College was difficult at first. After learning how to study, I was a solid student but not the stellar student that I was before in high school. At that time, I had some doubts whether I could withstand the rigorous challenge of medical school and residency. I was pretty much still undecided, even into my junior year. I still had to decide whether I would take the MCAT (Medical College Admission Test) and try to get into medical school or not. I went ahead and took the MCAT halfheartedly and did not do very well on the test. I applied to some medical schools but knew my chance of getting in was not good. It was around this time that my father died, midway through my senior year in college. I decided that I would go back to my hometown and live with my mother during this hard time for her. It was a blessing because it allowed me to get a job at the local hospital and to explore whether I wanted to pursue becoming a physician. It also allowed me to stay with my adoptive mother after the passing of my adoptive father. During that year, I still struggled with the idea of trying to become a physician. Being raised in a Christian home and seeing what my father did as a physician, I was asking God what he wanted to do with my life. I was taking the course to prepare myself for the upcoming MCAT test that I would retake. It took one hour each way to Columbus, Ohio, to reach my destination. I can remember clearly asking God for guidance and direction on one of my trips back and forth. There was no doubt that I received a message from him. It was strangely tranquil and peaceful when a thought came to me. This thought, which I believe was from God, told me that my purpose was to become a physician, similar to the great role models that I have had before me. I also had a sense of commitment to achieve this goal. I can remember telling myself, that I will become a physician at any cost, no matter how long it takes. It was at that moment that everything became focused and fell into place. I totally dedicated the rest of the time preparing for the MCAT and was ready to take the test when it came around.

The result of the change in my attitude was amazing. I had scored mediocre on the test before but now scored very high on the repeat test in all categories. It was unbelievable to realize that with my new scores, my chance of getting into medical school was significantly improved. In fact, I applied to six medical schools and received acceptance into all the schools. I decided to accept entry to Medical College of Ohio at Toledo. My best friend from childhood, Rodney Graber, was also accepted to attend. I graduated from medical school in the top half of my class. After deciding to pursue a career in emergency medicine, I applied and was accepted at the Methodist Hospital of Indianapolis, Indiana, one of the premier training centers in the country. I have never regretted my decision.

***

Rodney L. Graber, MD, FACC, Cardiology (Board Certified in Internal Medicine, Cardiology; Echo Cardiology: Nuclear Cardiology)

The Magnificent Oak Tree

My father has always loved trees, but one of his most favorites is the magnificent oak tree. When I look at an oak tree—its height, enormous width, colorful leaves, and deep roots—it mesmerizes me. The oak tree also exhibits an impressive ability to withstand various storms in life. Up in its branches, the fruit of the oak remains until they are overcome by gravity. The acorns depart from their origin and fall down, lying scattered on the ground underneath the canopy of the parental tree, each tiny acorn destined to become a magnificent oak tree. Just like all parents, the oak tree has packed its genetic information into each nut, supplying the biological instructions each acorn needs to grow into its destiny. Once on the ground, the acorn has to endure several external elements: worms, squirrels, and all four seasons of weather. If the acorn nut withstands these factors, it will be on its way to becoming an oak tree.

The genetic coding that God created in me through my mother and father was present in my chromosomes from the very beginning. Throughout my life, I have also encountered several environmental factors, but the worms, squirrels, and thunderstorms of my experiences sharpened me into who I am today. As I reflect on my journey to becoming a physician, I have realized that, perhaps, the acorn doesn't fall far from the oak tree after all.

The genetic package in me contained the biological instructions that I needed to grow, physically and mentally, as I traveled down the path toward becoming a physician. The information planted in the soil of my genome was furthered cultivated by the environmental factors of my childhood and young adulthood. The combination of what was planted by God, my parents, and those external elements has contributed to developing my traits of perseverance, integrity, compassion, and wonder, to name just a few.

The principle of "work before play" was woven into the fabric of my genome from the very beginning, intertwined with the principle of perseverance. My father strongly encouraged me to not quit anything that I started. Whether it was a project or a sport, I was encouraged to endure until the task at hand was completed. Weeding the garden, household chores, personal endeavors, and various school projects were all held to a high standard of excellence and perseverance. The time I left the basketball team in my junior year of high school proved to be a momentous event as this was the one and only time that I had made the conscious decision to quit something. Although my parents were probably disappointed at the time, I believe that they understood the circumstances surrounding the situation and supported me in my decision. The lessons that I learned from that experience and the counsel my parents provided helped build my understanding of "stick-to-it-ive-ness," and, to this day, I have endorsed and lived my life by the principle of perseverance because of it.

The simple phrase "Remember who you are," spoken by my father, embodies the definition I hold of "integrity." I often heard my father saying this, so much that if I were to walk through my childhood today, I would hear the same phrase echoing in the walls, embedded in the woodwork of each room. Not only did my father emphasize the importance of integrity during my childhood, but he also demonstrated it in his life every day, regardless of the "hat" he was wearing. I saw his example of integrity in all aspects of his life, from participating in and spectating sporting events, to engaging in several board meetings, to simply sitting at the dinner table. "Remember who you are" gave me the desire to preserve my family name but, more importantly, to honor God's name, setting the stage for a life of integrity. Even to this day, I feel honored to be known as Dr. Graber's son.

My mother demonstrated what it means to be compassionate on a day-by-day basis, from tending to my bumps and bruises, being there during my disappointed outcomes, and celebrating my joyous events. She taught me how to give good hugs and what it means to listen. Like my mother, my father also instilled compassion in me and was an excellent role model in this area, as well. I observed the compassionate behavior he had toward us, his children, as well as to the patients he took care of in his practice.

My father's character traits of perseverance, integrity, and compassion became even more evident in his life when my mother became ill several years ago. During that time, my mother became solely dependent on others for her care. My father was deeply rooted in the bedrock of his devotion to her and, like an oak tree, he weathered another storm planted firmly right by her side until her untimely death.

Throughout my life, even during the stormy season of my mother's passing in 2007, my father has always maintained a hunger for wonder and desire. As we walked down memory lane during her illness, I recall having various discussions with him while we were sitting at the dinner table or traveling in the car, talking in a way that fostered my wonder and desire to learn. During middle school and high school, I participated in various science fair projects that sharpened this attribute. As I reflect on those catalytic discussions, I recognize a common thread of scientific excitement revolving around ideas like Bernoulli's principle or Newton's laws. For example, my father explained the Bernoulli's principle to me in the car while we were on a family vacation. My father pointed out that the sensation that we felt when a semitractor trailer truck passed us on the highway, saying that we "felt" the pulling of the car because of Bernoulli's principle. Similarly, when my hat flew off of my head while riding a bicycle, I again learned about the Bernoulli's principle. With regard to Newton's law, my father would often say, "For every privilege there is an equal responsibility." I like to think that my father paraphrased Newton's Third Law, which states that "for every action, there is an equal and opposite reaction." My father's paraphrase nourished the principle of work before play, a lesson that remains valid for me today.

Prior to being a physician, my father enjoyed teaching. His obvious love for learning was grafted into my soul, for I too have a deep yearning to learn, and I wonder at the discovery of something new. When he taught me how to graft fruit trees in the spring and tap maple trees for maple syrup in the winter, I was fascinated. Both of these activities spawned ideas that led to some of my science fair projects that involved capillary reactions in trees and even testing the effects of steroids on plants. Other interesting science fair activities included testing the heat pump, generating electricity from windmills, and creating a biotin-deficient mouse. One of these science fair projects led me to the level of competition! My mother and father were proud of my accomplishment, and so was I. I know the wonder and desire to learn is contagious, even hereditary, for I have had the privilege to assist my own children with their learning from projects, too.

The genetic package contained within my acorn eventually took root, but I did not solidify the pursuit of medicine until my junior year in college—"a late bloomer," my father would say. All the while, environmental factors continued to act on my acorn, just as what happens in nature. I, too, had encounters with worm, squirrels, and all four seasonal changes. These helped to mold me into the physician I am today. The various successes and the failures in life, the challenging experiences, and the moments of joy have all acted upon my acorn, causing me to grow. I have grown and I continue to grow, eagerly pursuing wonder and the desire to learn.

Every seasoned physician will experience a variety of weather conditions during his or her medical career that will set the stage for both successes and failures. In the field of medicine, success is probably best defined by the eye of the beholder. I consider myself to be successful, but I learned from a number of self-identified failures, including subpar initial attempts to pass the required entrance tests. Repeating the MCAT exam led to a delayed admission to medical school. Initially, I was very disappointed, but, in retrospect, I am grateful for the extra time it took to gain admission as it further inspired the trait of perseverance in me. I had the privilege to attend Saint Louis University where my father attended medical school. I took postgraduate anatomy classes and excelled, reigniting my eagerness to learn at a much deeper level. I feel strongly that this experience propelled me to pursue a career in medicine. In fact, during one of my summer breaks in medical school, I had the great privilege to assist my father with one of his pacemaker surgeries! This experience provided the proper soil condition for the taproot of my young oak tree to nourish and grow. By the time I had completed medical school in 1993, I was in the top three of my graduating class. My success in medical school opened doors for entry into the University of Virginia internship and residency program, which I completed in 1996. My accomplishments there successfully opened doors at Ohio State University for entry into a cardiovascular fellowship program, which I completed in 1999.

I am now a licensed cardiologist and have had the privilege to work in the very practice that my father started in the early 1970s. Over the years, I have experienced both storms and sunshine, coping with multiple cases of patient death but also rejoicing with cases of physical healing. Within the first year of my career, I was struck with my first winter storm, a potential malpractice lawsuit. While this was a most unpleasant experience, it helped me prune some potential unhealthy branches of my oak tree and opened my mind to the medical-legal aspects of medicine. Fortunately, the case against me was dismissed and that experience spurred new growth for me in many ways. Largely because of that experience, I have felt motivated to serve on several hospital committees such as the Pharmacy and Therapeutics Committee, Ethics Committee, Medical Executive Committee, and Quality Peer Review and Quality Counsel Committees. Attending these meetings on a monthly basis has provided me with several career tools and served to develop both my personal and professional integrity.

I have now been practicing medicine for the past seventeen years. The majority of my patients are faced with the traditional triad of health issues: hypertension, hyperlipidemia, and diabetes. I would venture to say that several if not all of them have also encountered life's worms, squirrels, and adverse weather conditions. When I have sensed a challenge in my patient's life, being careful to ensure that it is appropriate, I have disclosed my winter storm experiences: my mother's death in 2007 and my failed marriage in 2012 and my faith's journey through each of the five stages of grief. Each patient with whom I have chosen to share my struggles has responded favorably, in turn being more open to sharing their own struggles with me. I have become a better listener and a more empathetic physician and, just as in nature, the warmth of spring always arrived after every bitter winter. I have been fortunate to be able to help my patients through both biological and emotional heart conditions since 2007.

Is one predestined to become a doctor? If I was, but ignored the different influences in my life, then I likely would not have become a physician, and I would not be in the place I am now, serving the patients as I do. Yes, I would have the same genetic makeup, but I would be "wearing a different hat." Being the little acorn that received that genetic makeup, paying attention to and weathering the different external factors of my environment and being blessed to have my father as a role model, I became the man that I am today.

So who am I and why am I a physician? I am a cardiologist, just like my father: my mentor and my friend.

I am the acorn that didn't fall far from the tree.

I am Dr. Graber's son.

CHAPTER 11

To Honor Where Honor Is Due

"Some people come into our lives and
quickly go. Some stay for a while and leave
footprints in our hearts and we are
never the same again." **K. Tribett**

Reflecting back to the beginning of my life's journey, in addition to my immediate family, four individuals, helped remind me of "the road less traveled" during my earlier medical career. The year was 1979. It was a time for special reflection upon my calling into medicine. I had received a surprising phone call inviting me to return to the teaching profession, to teach premedical students at Goshen College, the school where I received my undergraduate training. It was a moment of extraordinary excitement! That evening I shared this news with my family while sitting around the dinner table. I received two responses from the children. Cheryl, then a senior and Rhonda a junior in high school, shared their responses. Cheryl said, "I think you should pray about it, speak to some of your special friends and visit the college. Rhonda said nothing, but began to cry. The two boys provided no response and my wife agreed with Cheryl. Without a doubt, I was given profound wisdom!

I followed thru with the advice provided by my family. I spoke with Dr. Paul Hooley, the physician who had originally invited me to Logan County, Ohio. His immediate reply was, "I need you." Then I spoke to Reverend Howard Schmidt, a very caring gentleman, who said, "Maybe it's later than you think." Lastly, I spoke to my mentor and friend, Dr.

Charles Wooley and he replied without hesitation, "What you are presently doing is what you do best." The advice I received, put me at peace within and I did not pursue the matter any further. What I just shared set my "memory wheels" in motion, reflecting back upon certain individuals who had helped me in so many ways during my life time. It is for this reason I wish to dedicate this chapter to several of these special people.

My Mother

It was my mother, Anna Graber, who prayed for me during my early sick years and later the wayward years that definitely got my attention, one day, while picking pears. Though feelings of ambivalence of guilt and anger encompassed me for most of that historic day, it left an impact upon my life that never disappeared. If I have exhibited any characteristics of kindness, caring and love to others, I owe it to my mother. Thank you, Mother.

Mary Royer, PhD, Professor of Education

Dr. Royer was my favorite elementary education professor at Goshen College. The setting was immediately after I had dedicated my life to God, when she wrote me that historic but mysterious letter, saying, "I think God has something for you to do, other than being a teacher." Let me tell you, that hit me like a dart! Unfortunately, she didn't tell me what that "something" was. As the reader can recall, it took about five to six more years before I became quite burdened about the contents of that letter, but I knew for certain that I was being called into the profession of medicine. And it wasn't an easy path to travel. I packed two years of premedical science courses into one and one-half years. It became a path of life that I shall never forget but one that I thoroughly enjoyed. Medicine became my vehicle to care for patients for half a century. The reader has no idea how much I would like to travel that path of life again. For those who know me, medicine was just as exciting as golf, or maybe more! It was my calling. Thank you, Dr. Royer.

Paul Hooley, MD, Family Medicine

If it had not been for that "late call in the night" from DeGraff, Ohio, in 1965, I most likely would never have come to Bellefontaine, Ohio, to become a part of the medical community there. It was not my first or second choice, but it was that tired voice that I heard one night, at the eleventh hour, pleading for help. Even after agreeing to enter the practice of medicine in the Bellefontaine community, I experienced early ambivalence. The people of the community were very welcoming to my family and me, but the quality of medicine practiced raised early questions in my mind. Looking back upon those early years, I am thankful to Dr. Hooley for inviting me to this great community.

The late Dr. Hooley was very visionary in his thinking. He was probably the one most responsible in promoting the concept of establishing a medical clinic (1965) and bringing specialty physicians into Logan County. It was Dr. Hooley and several other physicians who carried out plans to construct a state-of-the-art intensive care unit in 1969. It was also Dr. Hooley who set up the Steps I and II exercise programs for post–heart attack patients, following the concept of Dr. Paul Douglas White. It was also Dr. Hooley who talked me into staying in this community when I was offered a position to teach premedical courses at a college. He was a very important physician for this community. Dr. Hooley, I thank you for inviting me to the great community of Logan County, Ohio. Once again, it was by *providence* that I received that "late call in the night." I made a good choice. The people of Logan County have become my people!

Charles F. Wooley, MD, FACC, Professor of Medicine, Division of Cardiology

The late Dr. Charles F. Wooley was the fourth person who had left a great impact upon my life. It was Dr. Wooley who made that second *providential* phone call to me, asking if I had ever considered furthering my training in cardiology. The setting was 1973. Being the only internal medicine consultant in Logan County, I soon became overwhelmed serving the medical needs of the local hospital, especially those patients with complicated heart problems. With that environmental setting, it didn't require much thinking to provide a response. So I replied, "I hadn't thought much about it, but it sounds quite interesting." (I had just become *board certified in internal medicine).* Accepting Dr. Wooley's invitation to go to the Ohio State University School of Medicine to enter the Cardiology Fellowship Training Program, was a *calling* I couldn't refuse. It fulfilled my dream! It also changed the path of my medical career. Not only was I able to remain in the great community of Logan County, but I also became connected with the Ohio State University

Division of Cardiology, allowing me to increase my depth of knowledge of medicine, especially cardiology. I met a lot of great physicians at the university, and I have much respect for every one of them. But it was Dr. Wooley who recognized me as a teachable student of medicine, providing me with the opportunity of my life. It is for this reason that I would like to share several worthy attributes, including other stories about my friend. A part of Dr. Wooley's life story will include those that have been passed on to me from his wife, children, "Profiles in Cardiology," and the Medical Heritage Center of the Health Science Library of the Ohio State University.

Life's Story

Charles F. Wooley was born in Jersey City, New Jersey. His father, from German-Irish stock, was a very energetic man who held a high position in the M. W. Oil Refinery Company. The family was of the Catholic faith. Charles graduated cum laude from Providence, Rhode Island (1950), where he met his future wife, Lucia. He attended and graduated from New York Medical College (1950–1954). After serving in the navy, he attended Ohio State University for his postmedical training in internal medicine and cardiology (1958–1963). He became the university's first director of the cardiac catheterization laboratory. Dr. Wooley authored and coauthored hundreds of scientific publications and received more *Teacher of the Year* awards than any other faculty member at the Ohio State College of Medicine from 1966–1981. According to the *Medical Heritage Center,* the last half of Dr. Wooley's academic career was devoted as a world-renowned medical historian. But according to his family and those close to him, he was deeply involved in medical research and writing medical history. He published multiple books, four of which were autographed and given to me. One book, *Academic Heritage: The Transmission of Excellence* is of special interest because in this book, special recognition was given to faculty leaders of the contemporary division of cardiology at Ohio State University.

Picture of Charles and Lucia Wooley

Historical Memories from Family

Lucia, Charles's wife mentioned, "Dr. Wooley looked upon and lived medicine as more than a profession, but as a vocation, in the religious sense. He was a perfectionist when it came to caring for his patients and teaching."

Steve Wooley, the youngest of the five children, gathered information from his siblings and passed it onto me. This is what he shared: "Dad had a tremendous influence on us." The paternal grandfather, also named Charles, was a gregarious, outgoing man whose extroverted nature belied a very serious appreciation for the natural world. This trait "rubbed off" onto his son, Charles F. Wooley. Not only did they go fishing together, but the grandfather also imparted to him an appreciation for natural ecosystems—no trip was complete without a discussion of the fact that larvae in the stream and pond beds fed all the creatures up to and including the game fish for which they angled. Steve goes on to say that this influence was passed on to him and his siblings and that many of their outdoor outings included a discussion of some topic involving natural history.

Sr. Elizabeth Walter of Saint Mary High School was Dr. Charles Wooley's biology teacher. She was strict and demanding and kindled a love for the natural world within my father. Personality-wise, she was a stark contrast to his father. Her focus with her students was driving home the importance of the scientific method while cultivating a love for biology. She focused upon the importance of observation to her students. As a result of her teaching, Dr. Wooley passed onto his children that while appreciation of the natural world was important, it was far more valuable if you understood what you were actually seeing. Dr. Wooley shared with his children how he had to stay after school to complete certain high school labs, because Sr. Elizabeth Walter didn't think his observations were precise enough to draw a conclusion. Steve went on to say that his father made sure that all his children met Sr. Walter during their lifetime.

It was also Sr. Walter who steered Dr. Wooley toward Providence College, in Providence, Rhode Island. Providence University at that time was mostly staffed by Catholic priests of the Dominican order, also known in short as "Order of the Preachers." It was this exposure with the Catholic professors that proved highly influential in directing him toward medical school.

Chris B. Wooley, third child of the family, also known as "the writer of the family," had this to share from his memoirs, entitled, *The Bigger Picture* (2008):

Our late father, Charles F. Wooley, MD, spent almost his entire career as a physician at Ohio State University. It was only natural that our family would become huge Buckeye fans—which we remain today. Dad played football growing up in North Jersey in the '40s against stiff competition, including their rival high school, St. Cecilia's, then coached by Vince Lombardi.

Dad learned and later taught us children that being a true sportsman wasn't just about winning. He knew that success usually followed those who had the courage to excel and who were committed to giving way more than the bare minimum. Dad always saw the bigger picture.

We spent many wonderful times in 'The Shoe' during the '60s and '70s. Dad appreciated a well-played game but always kept it in perspective. He knew that sports were an important part of college life but remained supremely loyal to the university as an institution of higher learning. When he heard that athletes received perks—travel, meals, scholarships— it sometimes frustrated him because of his overwhelming devotion to his students. They were never treated to steak dinners or bowl game trips. Dad believed that Ohio State University was all about educating young people and, in his case, training them to diagnose and cure diseases and save lives. He didn't begrudge athletes their perks, but he saw the bigger picture and thought the university should also acknowledge and support star students as tenaciously as they promoted Heisman Trophy contenders.

For a short time, Dad took care of Coach Hayes when Woody initially experienced heart problems. Although Dad admired Coach Hayes, both men were strong-willed individuals, and it wasn't long before Coach Hayes was seeing another physician in the Cardiology Division. I later understood there had been some sort of difference of opinion between them. I suspect that either Dad wasn't willing to treat Coach Hayes differently than any other patient, or that Woody had his own ideas about what should be done, or maybe both. Equality, fairness, and doing the right thing were not conceptual abstractions that Dad could compromise because his patient was famous. He lived those values daily in the Cardiology Division for his students to emulate and at home for his children to model.

Even though Coach Hayes was not his patient for very long, I remember one anecdote Dad shared about Woody that spoke volumes about both men. An OSU Athletic Department member fell ill one autumn Friday, and Dad saw him and recommended emergency heart surgery. The operation took place on Saturday morning, and naturally the patient missed the big football game, a road win over Illinois. Dad was up early Sunday morning and went to the hospital to check on his patient. Not many people got to the hospital before Dad. To his surprise, there was an autographed football on the table next to the patient. Woody had returned from Chicago, arrived at the hospital before Dad, and had dropped off the game ball. Dad remarked how impressed he was that Coach Hayes would go out of his way like that to cheer up a patient. Coach Hayes saw the bigger picture.

This past October I flew from my home in Anchorage to visit our mother in Columbus and attended the Penn State night game at 'The Shoe.' It was my first game since Dad died suddenly last February. The raucous crowd was as fired up as 105,658 people could be. During the pregame ceremony, when we sang 'Carmen Ohio,' tears streamed down my face as I remembered Dad. *'A joy which death alone can still...'* The fans around me sang passionately—as they always do—while I choked on the words. Later, after an infamous fumble sealed the Buckeyes' fate, many of the fans around me were deflated, upset, and angry at the loss. I looked around the beautiful stadium as Coach Tressel and the Buckeye players sang 'Carmen Ohio' in the chilly darkness of the south end of the stadium below me. This time I smiled and sang my heart out.

It was a disappointing loss, but it wasn't the end of the world. Instead, there was joy in returning to Columbus and being with my mother and friends. Our lives are short. We only get a brief ride on this spinning planet Earth. Of all the places in the endless universe, there I was standing near the top of the C-deck singing for my Dad. *'Time and change will surely show . . .'* Dad had raised a loving family. He touched—and saved—many lives and taught others the sacred gift of healing. For a brief moment, I gazed across the silhouette of University Hospital on the skyline and recalled how small and far away it used to seem when I was younger. In that instant I realized that as a child I could only see so much, but because of Dad, the bigger picture was in view.

Chris B. Wooley
November 22, 2008

I don't know how much you, being a bystanding reader, were touched by the stories that were shared from the family members. But in the event you were not emotionally moved, perhaps you didn't quite have a grasp of the bigger picture that was being told. As for me, parts of the missing puzzle that were woven into the person of Charles F. Wooley but not understood by many have been found—the early exposure of his father and his outstanding teachers from high school and college—became an integral part of his life. Because of those valuable environmental experiences, Dr. Wooley became that inquisitive and scientific person whom many of us observed and learned from. Now, I too, begin to see *the bigger picture* of the man who taught us so well. Keeping in mind what I had just shared, I invite you to learn some other traits of this intriguing gentleman—his deep interest in people—and his caring and compassionate attitude toward others.

As mentioned above, Dr. Wooley took a deep interest in people. It so happened I became one of those invested persons. I am not certain how the relationship began, but in retrospect, I recall that he showed a noticeable liking to me, even during my cardiology training years. Already then he was quoted as saying, "Dr. Graber burns with a blue flame." Among other things, there was a spiritual quality observed about him. This relationship grew to include both our families. We had similar interests in the outdoors, especially fishing and hiking in the woods. I was already living on a farm that included thirty-five acres of wooded land. Within the wooded area was a small fishing pond and cabin, which I named *Benjamin Pond* and *Edna's Cabin*—named after my father and my wife's (Roberta) mother. It resembled *Henry David Thoreau's* cabin. This became the original recreational ground for our two families, especially the men folks. Every autumn and early winter, we would go there to enjoy the recreation of cutting up fallen dead trees to be used as winter fuel for our homes. At noon we would take a break and sit inside the cabin to eat the warm lunch and drink the hot chocolate that Roberta had prepared for us. These were times well spent—just to be together and to watch the younger fellows flex their muscles—using the axe and chainsaws.

One evening, I was approached by a gentleman from Logan County who wanted to sell a large acreage of land to me. He brought several photos of the property with him. The parcel was mostly wooded and included a small lake. I shared this information with my new friend, Dr. Wooley. He immediately said, "We've got to buy it!" Up to this time, I didn't really know the depth of Dr. Wooley's compassion for nature, especially the attraction for wildlife, ponds, and forests. After further discussions, we, along with several other families, purchased the land. It included 120 acres of woods and a ten-acre lake. The lake was stocked with mature fish, including largemouth and smallmouth bass, and bluegills. Within the woods, we discovered multiple deep ravines and an old foundation what was thought to be one of the first one-room schools of Logan County. Within one main ravine flowed a shallow stream (we later learned, beneath this stream flowed a deeper, major stream that emptied into a natural lake, located about two miles east of our new property). Our first project was to blaze multiple walking trails so we could have better access to the different parts of the wooded acreage. Some years later, the group purchased an additional eighty-acre parcel of farmland that adjoined the original property. It included some woods also. It was a treasure! The properties were named *Pines Lake* I and II. We eventually constructed a beautiful cabin. This became the main site for our family gatherings—a heated cabin with inside plumbing (no television), many well-kept walking paths, a lake for fishing and ice skating, and excitement for hiking in the woods on a cold winter day!

Picture of Benjamin Pond and Edna's Cabin

For me and especially Charles, a walk in the woods was not only for hiking but also about intentional learning; why some trees thrived in certain areas but not in others—discovering different species of smaller plants—spotting wildlife, including muskrats, wild geese, mallard ducks, wild turkeys, great horned owls, white tail deer, etc. Sometimes, to enhance our learning, we would invite Mr. Bartlett, a professional forester, to walk with us. This took us one notch above merely admiring the beauty. Unless one has hiked in the woods with a professional forester, one has no idea how enriching the experience can be. One day, when touring the Pines Lake woods with Dr. Wooley and Mr. Bartlett, we were given an in-depth educational tour of plant life. We didn't walk great distances, but we covered much "scientific territory." I wished I had brought a pad and pencil along with me. Much of what was said sort of passed above me without much entry into my brain. We walked rather slowly and many times stopped just so we could focus upon what was being lectured to us. Along the way, the forester would stop and drill a small hole into a tree to assess the condition of its growth. He also explained why certain species of trees thrived in a certain type of soil and not others, etc. At one location of the woods, he was attracted to find some *quaking aspen* trees. He said he was surprised to find them growing in this part of the country. I never inquired, but I am almost certain this one particular hike made Dr. Wooley's day. And I'd bet it brought back vivid memories of the teaching he had received under the umbrella of the great Sr. Elizabeth Walter, teacher of his high school biology class. Our hikes in the woods were always focused upon learning something new about its environment. I don't recall that we ever walked just for the sake of physical exercise. However, we did get an excessive amount of exercise because of its size and interesting terrain. More than once we found ourselves hiking in directions different from what was planned. (We apparently forgot to note that the fungus always grows on the north side of a tree.) Our hikes were precious, too, for we were entering into the territorial community that the different mammals, amphibians, reptiles, and birds claimed as their home. We were cognizant that we were hiking in a special territorial spot of God's great creation. On a separate day, when I was walking through the white pine section of the woods, I stumbled onto a pinecone. It had ten little pine seedlings attached to it. It reminded me of a mother hen huddled around her tiny chicks. I saved a few of the seedlings for my friends and planted the rest in the surrounding fertile, moist soil.

Springtime also became an interesting adventure for the male figures of the Wooley and Graber families. We became quite interested in the preservation of trees, so we began to plant tree seedlings. We planted seedlings by the thousands! We would follow the guidelines as provided by our forester. We learned it was more complicated than just to learn how plant the seedlings. The larger problem was how to protect them from wildlife, especially the deer and rodents. It was expected that about one-half of the seedlings would survive. Today, if one walked where we planted the tree seedlings, one would find many that became adult trees. From these experiences, we learned the importance of preserving the trees of God's planet Earth. Like the trees, the seeds of friendship between the two families continued to grow.

Lest the reader asks, "What does this have to do with the making of a physician?" Well, it contributes much! We physicians also require time away from our daily responsibilities. Not only does it release us from our daily stresses of work, but it leads to something much greater and more lasting. For the Wooleys and the Grabers, it brought together two families of different social environments, to become lasting friends from that time forth. It provided opportunities to share our personal, social, and spiritual values with each other. In so doing, we developed a deep caring for one another, just as the Great Physician intended it to be.

I remember the last walk in the woods that Dr. Wooley and I had together. It was a very worthwhile walk, but it was different. This time, I noticed it required much more effort for my friend to walk the winding paths we normally took. Usually when we came to a given fence, we would climb over it and continue our scientific journey. But this time, Dr. Wooley required assistance to climb the fence. I remember asking him if he was all right, and he answered, "I'm okay." Although he shrugged it off, I remained concerned.

I visited my friend at the Ohio State East University following his hip surgery two days before his untimely death. He shared different things with me; some things were about *Pines Lake* property. Then he changed the subject and stated that he had noticed having a "run of a ventricular arrhythmia" on his monitor. This was two days before his sudden death.

I was extremely saddened learning of those recent events. We had developed a very close friendship with each other. We freely talked about many things, including spiritual matters. I remember he and Lucia attending my wife's (Roberta) funeral in 2007. Their presence meant so much to me at that time. Although they were representatives from a different denomination, we gathered together that day as one body of Christ's church. I remember afterward, we spoke of the importance of all Christians (irrespective of denominational differences) needing and supporting each other. Dr. Wooley was not only my mentor in cardiology medicine; I also claimed him as my brother.

After Dr. Wooley's death, I was asked to participate at the Memorial Grand Rounds, in his honor, at Ohio State University. In closing, I will share my presentation, as a tribute to this great man and personal friend.

Charles F. Wooley Memorial Medical Grand
Rounds of Ohio State University

-----A Tribute----

There is something that is somewhat awkward about waiting to pay tribute to great mentors, as was Dr. Charles Wooley, until after they pass from this earth. It seems to me one should also pay tribute to these great people while they are still alive. It was providential that I was led to share my personal appreciation to Dr. Wooley about three months preceding his death—and I am thankful that I did, for he was extremely worthy of my expression of praise and honor to him.

I would like to briefly share several examples of tribute to this great professional gentleman:

(1) The late Dr. Francis Peabody once said, "The best care one can give a patient is to care for that patient." Dr. Wooley not only passed this concept on to me, but I also observed him to personally care for every patient I referred to him. My patients always felt he provided them with a quality of expertise in a very caring manner. I remember wanting to refer a patient to him from Bellefontaine, Ohio, who had developed a dynamic mitral regurgitant murmur following an acute myocardial infarction. And he said, "Why don't I just come to Bellefontaine and see the patient there?" He drove sixty miles to care for this patient and never charged one cent.

(2) Dr. Wooley was a master artist. He had a unique gift of taking partially formed pieces of "human clay" and reshaping that clay into finely polished vessels. Like many of you sitting in this audience, Dr. Wooley took me and reshaped me into the person and cardiologist I am today. In 1973, having just passed my internal medicine boards, Dr. Wooley said to me, during a phone

conversation, "Have you ever considered getting more training in cardiology?" That question of personal interest not only paved the way for my entry into the cardiology training program at Ohio State University but also initiated a community cardiology program at Mary Rutan Hospital of Bellefontaine that was unlike any other its size in the state of Ohio. Reshaping and polishing pieces of "human clay" into finely polished vessels was his calling.

(3) Dr. Charles Wooley was a very meticulous and artful scientific investigator and motivator. It was my privilege to have been trained under his umbrella, beginning in 1974. As a special project of my clinical cardiology training, I was asked to review five or six medical records of patients from a given community who had similar cardiology problems. I remember him handing me those patient records, saying, "I don't know, but I have a hunch these patients are of the same family, with similar cardiac problems." Then he asked me to investigate this matter. When asked what literature I should review to find the answer, he replied, "There is no published literature. It is your job to find out." As you now know, this was the beginning of an extensive ongoing investigation, now led by Libby Sparks, et al., covering more than nine generations of a family with heritable myocardial and conduction system disease, which included the discovery of "Lamin A/C Cardiac Conduction and Myocardial Disease."

(4) "You can have your cake and eat it too." Dr. Charles Wooley was not only my professional mentor, but we and our families became long-lasting friends. We have many precious memories to share. A few include working in the woods on a cold wintry and snowy day, splitting wood, and taking time out to eat warm lunch in a *Henry David Thoreau*–styled cabin at *Benjamin Pond*—the planting of hundreds and hundreds of tree seedlings—or even attending a three-day forestry course put on by OSU Extension, Dr. Wooley and I being the only ones not to receive a diploma. There are many memories involving these two families.

In closing, there is a lesson for the wise—say a special thanks to your mentors for the training and reshaping of your lives, while those persons are still alive. And to you, the family of Charles F. Wooley, thank you for the invested years your loved one shared with me.

Harry. L. Graber, MD, FACC
June 23, 2008

In conclusion, one of the benefits to glean from these persons of honor, is to learning and appreciating the importance of environmental factors which influence all of us. It is my hope you will reflect upon your own past providential experiences and consider them when choosing the path of life to be traveled.

CHAPTER 12

Other Expectations of Physicians in a Rural Setting

A friend and former medical colleague said at the time
of his retirement, "There is life beyond medicine." While
that is true, there are also other assignments, which may
or may not be associated with direct medical care—
waiting for physicians to provide leadership within the
community where he/she resides.

Additional Expectations of Physicians—Medical Center vs. Rural Setting

While I cannot attest to what accounts for all extracurricular (e.g.,
activities beyond direct care for patients) responsibilities of physicians at
large medical centers, I do know much of their additional professional
responsibilities involve performing diagnostic testing, student teaching,
research, and scientific presentations (conferences). This is in contrast
to extracurricular responsibilities of physicians in rural settings. The
primary responsibility of physicians in a rural setting is to provide direct
care of his/her patients. Those who are subspecialists, though they may
provide less direct patient care, become responsible as consultants to
primary care providers, as well as perform and interpret specific medical/
surgical procedures. Less time would be devoted to teaching or directing
educational meetings. Physicians living in a rural environment frequently

become involved with additional community issues that may or may not pertain to the profession of medicine.

I have always felt some responsibility to volunteer myself to assist in certain areas of medical and educational needs within the community I reside. With my earlier professional background in education and later medicine, there were numerous opportunities to become involved. Some years ago, I was invited to serve on the Logan County Health Board. Not only did I feel I could make a positive contribution, but I also felt it to be a civic obligation to serve the community in this capacity.

The local health district assumes much responsibility monitoring the health needs and sanitation issues within the county, making sure the community maintains high health standards at every level. A main theme might be "to serve as a preventive for widespread diseases." That statement encompasses many issues: sanitation, monitoring health standards in restaurants and motels, monitoring established regulations for disposing refuse, providing immunizations (preventive for contagious diseases), delivering medical care, and the list goes on. Local health districts play a very important role in every community and every state of our nation. To become better informed, I would recommend a member of every family to attend your local health board meeting at least once, to gain a better insight and appreciation of its important functions. I am much indebted and grateful to this organization and the work they do. If you should ever be privileged to travel to some of the underprivileged countries where poor sanitation is the norm, you would understand why those same places are infested with many contagious diseases. I have visited some of these places and will share more in detail in another chapter. Be thankful and supportive for the local and state healthcare organizations, especially our *Logan County Health District.*

Healthcare professionals (physicians, etc.) may be called to participate in providing annual physical examinations on school athletes. I was privileged to volunteer my services at our local school of West Liberty/ Salem for a number of decades. This has been an important healthcare assignment, as I not only screened for potential physical abnormalities, but I was also provided the opportunity to learn about the person. Invariably I would ask how the student was doing in school—what they liked best about school, what their favorite subject was, what they wished to do with their life. I would also frequently ask them which foreign language they were taking. This gave me a clue as to how studious they were (Spanish language seems a little easier to grasp than French). Medicine became my "vehicle" to reach out to the student.

I made it my responsibility to stay close to all facets of education of the local school district, irrespective of the function—remember, I was also a teacher during my earlier years. It was my privilege to serve on the local *board of education* for seven years. This enhanced my efforts to remain close to the educational and extracurricular functions of the school and community. I have continued to follow some of the major sport events at West Liberty Salem School; participation in sports can become a positive environmental experience of life. I have, over the years, spoken or written to different athletes, some letters of encouragement and others letters of praise. Below is an example of one of those letters written on July 15, 2014:

> Dear . . . ,
>
> First, my congratulations to you for your most recent achievement as a graduate of the *United States Air Force Academy!*
>
> I first took notice of you during your high school years, especially on the basketball court. I recall you being "ruffled up" many times by opposing players. Yet I never saw you lose your cool. You kept your focus upon what you needed to do as a team player.
>
> I was greatly impressed! From those observations and others, I was convinced you had received quality instructions from home, your church, and people of this great community. You portrayed a message of hope, a message much like my own. However, what appears different for the two of us, is that your course in life is *futuristic,* whereas mine has been mostly traveled . . . with excitement! Near completion! Mine reflects memories, and yours remains to be traveled . . . yet we both share a common denominator. It begins with a dream that becomes a reality, and God, if He allows it, will lead the way!
>
> A friend forever!
>
> Harry L. Graber, MD

Physicians may also be asked to present certain health issue topics to different club functions. It has been my privilege to participate at this level numerous times during my medical tenure. A special privilege has been to serve multiple terms on one or several of the local boards of Mary Rutan

Hospital. This provided me with a valuable insight into the administrative function and its role in providing health care.

Many people of all communities not only become leaders of civic organizational functions but also play leadership roles in local churches. Years ago, I was asked to become the Sunday School superintendent of the church I attended. Having had earlier training and experience of a school teacher, I was sensitive to the need for learning. I had a suspicion that the church membership was not too well informed about the Bible. So to test whether or not my suspicion was correct, I ordered a survey test from a Southern Baptist organization and had each attendee take this test. As one might suspect, the older population was the best informed, but the remainder of the congregation did not perform as well. This led to a very interesting project. It became an ecumenical (multiple church) church school project for learning, an organized program that met every Sunday night for many months. This became a very popular adventure that lasted at least a year or more. Attendance was unbelievably outstanding!

Comment: What does this have to do with being a physician? Probably very little, but to illustrate, like other professionals, physicians living in a rural community will be invited to assume leadership roles of one type or another, in addition to caring for the sick.

CHAPTER 13

Other Medical Stories and Events

Not all my life's adventures in medicine have been of a serious tone. Some displayed a hint of humor as well. This chapter will include a mixture of both. I will begin by sharing some of the lighter stories.

Stories Associated with "a Bit of Humor"

Soon after I had arrived to begin my first year of medical practice in Logan County, Ohio, I received a phone request from a family to make a "house call" on behalf of their father, who was experiencing abdominal pain—it was nighttime. I listened carefully for instructions to find the patient's house. Now, one has to know a little bit about some of the county and township roads in Logan County, Ohio, to appreciate my story. Many of these "off roads" were not easy to find, especially at night. I'm not certain, but I have a hunch these roads originated from earlier *Shawnee American Native* trails. They were winding and narrow and poorly marked—and at night almost impossible to identify. Why, one could easily get lost! And that's exactly what happened to me. Not only did I not find where this ill gentleman lived; I also had much difficulty finding my way out of the territory. I spent a couple of hours trying to locate where this man lived. I never did have the privilege seeing this patient. To this day, I do not know what happened to this gentleman. I followed the nightly newspaper to see if he was named in the *obituary column*, but he could not be found there either. Maybe he was experiencing a bit of indigestion, or even constipation. I'm hoping whatever it was "passed" through his intestinal tract without major complications.

A second interesting story was about a patient known as Mrs. Brown. Now, I always review the patient's medical record before entering into an examining room. To complicate this incident a little bit, I should tell you that I had been caring for two elderly couples whose last name was Brown. As I opened the door, I said, "Good afternoon, Mrs. Brown. How are you feeling today? And how is your husband doing?" The patient was startled and then replied, "Why Dr. Graber, my husband has been gone for five years!"

An elderly lady came to see me in my medical office one day. She was a native of Logan County but had moved to Arizona. Apparently she had returned to Logan County to visit her family, and while here, she made an appointment for a routine checkup. When I entered the examining room, we greeted each other, and then she promptly said, "Why, Dr. Graber, you look so young and healthy!" Playing the "light talk game," I mistakenly asked, "Well, how old do you think I am?" She said, "Oh, about seventy-three." I was still in my mid-sixties. I must have had a bad day that I appeared so old.

As a cardiologist, my routine was to spend quality time with each of my patients. I would carefully ask the appropriate questions and perform a thorough cardiac examination. But this elderly lady was an exception. She always anticipated more than an updated heart evaluation. She expected a manicuring procedure, too. No, not the fingernails, but her toenails. Being the kind of a person I am, I would get down on my knees and trim her toenails. It was sort of a ceremonial "demonstration of humility," like a "foot washing" ceremony in church. I never advertised this service to anyone else.

One weakness of my medical career was forgetting to submit patient service charges to the front office. I was frequently reminded I would "go broke" if it wasn't for them. The patient I'm about to share with you was one of those forgetful billing moments. An elderly gentleman presented himself to the emergency room in complete heart block (a blockage of electrical conduction where the conduction pathway of the upper chambers become separated from the lower chambers, causing the ventricles to contract very slowly in an unstable manner). Suddenly the man's heart stopped completely, requiring immediate intervention. Fortunately, I was able to quickly insert an electrical electrode into the right lower chamber (cavity of right ventricle) and attach it to a temporary pacemaker, saving the gentleman's life. The patient soon underwent a permanent pacemaker implant, and from his perspective, "he was as good as before," Much technical time and expertise had been spent on this gentleman's life-threatening problem. Months later, the man came to me to thank me for saving his life and not charging him for my service.

A middle-aged man was admitted to ICCU from the hospital emergency room with chest pain. He had advanced obstructive coronary artery disease with a history of previous heart attacks. He also had a long history of tobacco abuse including up to the present time. While the nurses were attending the patient, starting intravenous lines, etc., he suddenly developed a rapid ventricular tachycardia with profound hypotension. Immediate cardioversion was successfully performed—not enough time to premedicate the patient. He called out with a boisterous voice, "I'm sorry, Doc. I promise, I will quit smoking!"

Adventures to Other Countries on Short Mission Assignment

During the hospital administrative tenure of the late Ewing Crawfis, Harold Martin, a former Bellefontaine high school superintendent, Dr. Glen Miller and I became interested in a mission outreach assignment in the Central American country of Belize. This led to an acquaintance with YWAM (Youth with a Mission), a nondenominational international organization whose presence was known in that country. With hospital sponsorship, a respiratory therapist, my wife, Roberta, and I flew to Belize to provide a short-term medical service. Mr. Gascho took a portable ECG machine along, and I served as a cardiology consultant to the internal medicine specialist of Belize City, the capital of the country. While there, we evaluated numerous patients, one with congenital heart disease (atrial septal defect) and several afflicted with advanced *valvular heart disease*, secondary *rheumatic fever*. Preliminary arrangements were made to have one patient transferred to the United States. While in the capital city, I was privileged to make hospital medical rounds with the native internal medicine specialist. I consulted on a Catholic nun who had been hospitalized with a rapid sinus tachycardia, which turned out to be secondary to hyperthyroidism. Immediate treatment included usage of *propranolol and* propylthiouracil. Plans were made to transfer the patient back to the United States for definitive treatment. This proved to be a worthy mission assignment for the three of us. I was impressed with the internal medicine physician. He was quite knowledgeable. Unfortunately, the hospital was in need of considerable repair and lacked the necessary modern technology needed to provide better patient care. The library was also lacking in the latest textbooks and journals. It was a very worthwhile experience, and I was glad we could be of help.

I served two short-term mission assignments with *Mercy Ship Ministries,* Sierra Leone, in 1993 and Benin in 1997, both West African countries. In preparation for my first assignment, my wife and I visited the *Anastasis* in 1992 (a vessel owned by *Mercy Ship Ministries*) while it was docked along the coastal region of France. We were much impressed with the tour and the outstanding work being carried out by this organization. Before leaving, I committed to my first (one month) term assignment in the fall of 1993, in Sierra Leone, West Africa. (Sierra Leone is the home country of Albert Massaquoi, who shared his story in chapter X of this book.)

Photo of Albert Massaquoi of Sierra Leone, West Africa –volunteer interpreter For Dr. Graber at Mercy Ships out patient clinic.

Mercy Ship Ministries (MSM) is a nationally known organization whose headquarters are located in Texas. MSM was founded by Donald Stephens in 1978, who remains president of the organization. It originally was under the umbrella of YWAM (Youth with a Mission). In 1993, MSM owned about three ships, *Anastasis* being the largest of the three, and spent most of its active years along the coastal countries of Africa. The ship was retired in 2007. The next paragraph will describe more about the ship and the MSM program.

Mercy Ship Vessel (Anastasis) along the coast of Sierra Leone, West Africa

The *Anastasis* was a fairly large vessel, measuring over five hundred feet in length and having nine decks. It was equipped with three surgical suites and three additional rooms—a dental clinic, an X-ray unit, a laboratory, and forty patient beds. It contained many private quarters for families living on the ship; a school for the children of the families living on the ship; and a chapel, which was used for worship services, evangelism teaching, and other meetings as needed from time to time. It had a large dining room and kitchen. In a lower deck were laundry facilities for all occupants of the ship. Air conditioning was limited to the surgical suites. The living quarters for the volunteer workers were small. Each unit was supplied with a fan, lavatory, a small desk and chairs, and two bunk beds. With no air conditioning, the rooms remained very hot at night until after about eleven o'clock.; I am certain the newest ship is completely air-conditioned. Each volunteer is responsible for his/her own expenses during the duration of their assignment.

Before arrival to the designated country, an advanced team of workers would go to the given area to perform massive screening examinations on prospective surgical patients. Flyers would be posted before the ship's arrival and also handed out to the native people to inform them of the ship's arrival date.

Multiple programs were carried out on each *Anastasis* adventure. Some included the provision of medical care to "on land" outreach clinics and in hospital medical/surgery care, plus dental clinics. Typical surgical procedures included removal of benign facial and neck tumors of viral etiology, cleft palate repairs, correction of strabismus (cross-eyed), cataract surgery, orthopedic surgery, etc. Additional services included agriculture, health education, developmental projects, drilling wells for water, mental health programs, etc.

My assignment in Sierra Leone and Benin, for the most part, was working with a team of physicians and nurses on land, in an outpatient clinic. All physicians were responsible in caring for the "whole person." Although my expertise was in the subspecialty of cardiology, it now became general medicine. Many times I wished I had paid more attention to *parasitology* (pertaining to parasites, viz. roundworms, tapeworms, malaria, etc.) when attending medical school.

The outpatient clinics were located several miles from the ship, in a rural setting where preconstructed shelters had already been set up for the outreach program. The large shelters consisted of spaced upright poles, with palm branches overhead, to protect everyone from the hot sun. A second, smaller shelter was constructed to serve as the pharmacy. Smaller petitions were constructed to serve as examining rooms; included were a few chairs and a simple exam table. Most of the pharmaceutical medicines were provided from Germany. From past experiences, the leadership knew what medicines were needed, but we often lacked certain kinds.

The natives were very appreciative of the medical care that was being provided for them. They would walk miles to be cared for at the clinic. Many were quite ill, some near death, wanting to receive healing. A very common complaint included chronic headaches—mostly secondary to chronic dehydration. The majority of the young children presented with enlarged spleen, secondary to malaria. Parasitic infestations from tapeworms (*platyhelminthic)* and roundworms (*Ascaris)* were common as were skin (scabies) and chronic ear infections with purulent drainage. Other diseases included tuberculosis, blindness (some secondary from infected flies, cataracts, Kwashiorkor disease, which is a chronic nutritional disease characterized by a lack of proteins and appropriate vitamins—with characteristic findings of abdominal distention, fine reddish hair, anemia, dark crumpled patches of skin over the knees, elbows, etc. I saw one child who had empyema associated with fistula drainage from the thorax.

Many of the disease entities mentioned above I had never seen. At one of the clinics, there was an outbreak of measles; one child died while at the clinic. I saw another patient who was infested with roundworms. He was very frail. While examining the boy, I could see movement of an ascaris under the skin of the abdomen. This boy also died at the clinic.

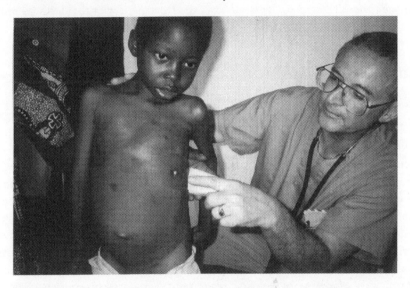

Examining a child with empyema with a fistulas drainage of the chest (pustular material)

Being away from family medicine for some time, I sought help from seasoned family physicians who had volunteered with *Mercy Ships* multiple times. They were well acquainted with most of the parasitic diseases. My expertise was mostly to help with the patients with cardiac problems. Not all the healthcare professionals were from the United States; there was a nice representation from different countries—a facet that made the work so fascinating.

One elderly lady (the average life span at that time was in the early fifties) whom I evaluated complained of dyspnea (shortness of breath) with exertion and findings of a heart murmur (murmur of aortic insufficiency). There was no evidence of peripheral edema of the legs (swelling from fluid) or basilar rales of the lungs (moister of lung bases). Neither did she have any jugular neck vein distention. But she did have a systolic pressure elevation with a decrease of the diastolic pressure. Unfortunately, appropriate heart medicines for this lady were quite limited. I did find a limited supply of *Cardizem* (a calcium-blocking agent) to give to the patient. The next day, this lady came back, wearing a beautiful flowered dress just to tell me "thank you." She said the shortness of breath was almost gone. Unfortunately, the medicine I prescribed would only help her for about six weeks. I thought about this patient many times; if only I could have referred her to a medical center to receive an aortic valve replacement! I felt the same about many of the other afflicted patients we saw; the treatment we provided was only temporary . . . and that was sad.

What Is Retirement?

Do you really want to know the meaning of retirement? *Merriam-Webster's Collegiate Dictionary* defines it as "an act of retiring; reserved; shy; withdrawn from one's position or from an active working life; a place of seclusion or privacy." Who wants to be secluded? I could accept it as being a transition from one's type of work to another. I "retired" six separate times, the final one being due to a sense of physical stress I had never experienced before; this time I knew my career was completed—I came to the end of my "continuum"! I have jokingly said the reason it took me six times to finally retire is because I'm a slow learner—I needed to keep repeating until I could "catch on" to the meaning of *retirement*. Another excuse I have given is, at the time of my first retirement, a surprise party was secretly planned for me. This included several hundred guests from different states, family members, and professors from Ohio State University. It was a formal occasion which included a banquet dinner, followed by guest speakers from the university. It was a class act! I never received so much attention in my life. My cardiology colleagues, who were responsible for the event, set up a special education fund at the university bearing my name. Well, that momentous occasion was so appealing, I thought I would keep repeating the retirement act! However, each time I repeated it, the less attention I received, so I finally gave up on the idea. No, none of this reasoning is true. Since the day I experienced the call into the medical profession, I have lived a very exciting professional life. There was no doubt in my mind this is where God wanted to use me. Medicine became *my vehicle* in caring for the sick. I loved it and would choose to walk the same path again. The following paragraphs include what I did after my initial retirement in 1991.

I was invited to replace Dr. Glen Miller as administrative medical director of Mary Rutan Hospital. I continued my assignment with the *Medical Education Committee* of Ohio State University as well as my *"OSU Family"* research on *heritable dilated cardiomyopathy and conduction disease.* I also continued serving as director of medical education at Mary Rutan Hospital. These remained my assignments for the rest of that decade.

One year following my second retirement, I was invited to set up an outpatient cardiology clinic for the Division of Cardiology at Ohio State University (OSU) East Hospital. This was to be a part-time assignment, allowing me to care for outpatients two half days per week. I was also asked to monitor and advise the outpatient cardiac rehab program; it included reviewing patient records, discussing the cases with the nurses, and providing a documentary note for the chart. This assignment began in 2001 and continued through mid-2007. It proved to be a rewarding experience for me. Most of the patients I had seen were referred to me from other physicians: referrals from within the city of Columbus as well from care providers sixty or more miles away. My referrals included patients from variable backgrounds, university professors, and those on welfare.

One patient who was referred to me was a prisoner who had developed severe leg edema secondary to congestive heart failure. I spent a lot of time with this gentleman. He took a liking to me, and that became the first step for him to seriously follow my medical advice. After three months of intense therapy and counseling, this gentleman lost about thirty pounds. Equally important was I was able to gain his confidence and trust. At the time of my departure, the patient was ready to be released from prison. I hope he continued in the right path of life.

A second patient, an attractive lady, presented to our clinic office with symptoms of chest pain. A male friend accompanied her. She was in her forties, of slender build, and measured about six feet in height (I most always would provide about one hour of my time with each patient during their first visit). Social habits included alcohol and tobacco abuse. She denied use of recreational drugs. The physical examination was unremarkable, but because of her symptoms of chest pain and abusive social habits, appropriate tests were ordered to exclude obstructive coronary artery disease. The patient was asked to return, following the tests, to go over the results and discuss the importance of a healthy lifestyle. On the return visit, I asked the patient "Where is your friend?" She replied, "We had a fight last night, and he was threatening me with a knife." This was an appropriate time to share some "heart to heart" counseling. I stated that all her studies were normal. I also commented that with her slender body build and height, she must have been an outstanding athlete in her younger days. She replied, "No, I was a street runner" (by this time I had become acquainted with some of that language). She cried and said, "I know better. I was raised in a good home and attended a Baptist church." I replied, "This is a good start, and it's not too late to make this important change in your life." The patient never returned, but I believe she was ready for a life-changing experience.

In the fall of 2007, I was invited to return to temporary part-time work at Cardiology Associates of Bellefontaine, Ohio (now an outpatient clinic of Ohio State University). It was good to return to the community where my medical efforts first began. My assignment lasted for about one year when the university was able to find a full-time nurse practitioner. Then another need arose at Mary Rutan Hospital.

My second-to-last cardiology assignment (2009) was spent in the outpatient clinic of Mary Rutan Hospital, caring for the indigent patients of our local community who were in need of cardiology services. This was a very attractive setting. I attended the clinic one day per week and was able to spend sufficient time with every patient. One patient commented, "No one has ever given me this much attention for my health problems as you have." But reality of the comment is, in today's setting, no practicing physician can afford giving this much attention and financially survive. I was just grateful that I could do this at this time of my life. Most of the patients I cared for were victims of disease caused by genetics; some combined with early abnormal social habits. I spent one year at this clinic, satisfied that I was able to provide quality care to this group of needy patients. At the time I had every intention that this would be my last cardiology assignment, but because of a shortage of help at one of Ohio State's cardiology clinics, I answered the call to help out one more time.

I anticipated that at the close of 2009 and the beginning of 2010 that my clinical years of medicine in cardiology were moving swiftly toward the completion of my career. I was given an *emeritus status* from the Division of Cardiology at Ohio State University. One year later, I received an *emeritus status* from the State Medical Board of Ohio. Although my active medical practice came to a close, I continued to keep up with reading medical literature. I was enjoying my hobbies of gardening and golf. I felt very satisfied that I had given my best to the profession of medicine for approximately one-half of a century. But as time went on, I wondered if I had submitted my state license prematurely. It seemed quite difficult for me to come to terms with the decision I had made. There was a feeling of emptiness within my soul. I despised the concept of *retirement!*

One would think this was going to be the end of my medical career, but not so. It was May of 2014 when I received a call from my dear friend and colleague, Dr. Evan Dixon—*"third call in the night."* He had been working tirelessly at the Ohio State University Heart Clinic of Cambridge, Ohio, *burning both ends of the candle.* He called, asking if I would be willing to return to work to help him out. To this day, I don't know why, but there was an inner spark of excitement when he addressed that question to me. The spark, however, did not create a flame, for I no longer had an active medical license, and I would need to update my CME credits to obtain one. Being away from the medical world for a couple of years, I would need to enroll in a quality review course of cardiology. All these thoughts circulated in my mind. I needed some quality time to think and pray about it, and that is how I left it with my friend.

After I gathered my composure and had time to consider all the questions I had raised, I told Dr. Dixon I would consider helping at the Cambridge Cardiology Clinic if the university would assist in having my state license reinstated. In the meantime, I began studying and updating my CME credits. Within several months, I had fulfilled the CME requirements and received notice that my license was reinstated. I enrolled in a cardiology board review course at the Cleveland Clinic and began the process for a medical staff reappointment with the Division of Cardiology at Ohio State School of Medicine. The entire process took about four months of hard work. My application was finally accepted and approved by Ohio State University. I began my part-time work at the OSU Heart Clinic of Cambridge, Ohio, in November 2015. Because I had not been in active practice of cardiology medicine for several years, my work was being monitored for the first four to six weeks. I felt very prepared scholastically, to perform my duties without difficulty. The only drawback, however, was learning and getting used to the *electronic billing* that had become mandatory by the U.S. government. Fortunately, I had an outstanding nurse who was well trained for the new adventure of billing. Technically, she was known as a *"scribe."* To assure that my patients were getting 100 percent of my attention, I would briefly explain the necessity of the newly established burden that was placed upon us and would verbalize my findings so they, too, would be able to know what I was thinking. I always provided special time for explaining my thoughts and findings, often using illustrated wall charts of heart models to accomplish that goal. I welcomed my patients' questions, wanting to make sure they understood me. I performed complete physical examinations. More than once, I discovered abnormal physical findings, unrelated to cardiovascular problems. My goal was to care for the patient; that was my responsibility.

I worked at the Ohio State University Heart Center in Cambridge, Ohio, for nine months—a commitment to provide quality care to the patients of that community until a permanent replacement could be found. I had nothing but praise for all the healthcare staff who were employed at the clinic; they were a great staff—well trained, friendly, and caring! Disadvantages of this work assignment were several. Traveling to work was stressful and tiring. It required about two and a half hours of travel time from my home near West Liberty, Ohio, to Cambridge, Ohio. I worked half a day on Mondays, stayed at a motel overnight, and worked another half day on Tuesday, then traveled back to my home late afternoon. I would be provided with copies of medical records to take home with me to review and prepare for the next week of work. This was not a casual task. Many of the records were voluminous and complex to review, requiring three to four hours of preparation time.

The people of the Cambridge community were very delightful to care for; most presented with multiple and complex medical problems. This required much time and effort on my part. For example, I needed to make certain that prescribing a drug beneficial for the heart of a given patient would not become detrimental to another organ such as the kidneys, for most of the elderly patients had multiple organ diseases. Probably the most difficult problem for me to adapt to was that I did not know any of the physicians of the Cambridge community. I could tell from the patients who were referred to me that they had been given excellent care, but becoming acquainted with the medical professionals would have been of much help to me.

Not being familiar with people of a given community can be an initial disadvantage for the patient and the care provider alike. It requires months for the feeling of trust to develop. But for some reason, I didn't experience this adverse feeling at Cambridge. Everyone was quite receptive and respectful! Example two: I was scheduled to see a patient in consultation because of a reported abnormal nuclear stress study. The patient was recommended to have a heart catheterization to exclude obstructive coronary artery disease. Before agreeing to the request, he was asking for a second opinion. I had reviewed the patient's medical record the night before his appointment. It was as thick as a *Sears and Roebuck Catalog*. Upon review, I noted he had had many medical problems of the past. He was unemployed and was on Medicaid. He was in his mid-forties. I also noted the patient had been fully employed but, because of past injuries, was on disability.

As I entered the examining room the next morning, I was greeted by a delightful gentleman and his wife. He said he wanted a second opinion before submitting to a recommended heart catheterization. I carefully listened to his history of chest pain and reviewed the nuclear stress study with him, using the wall chart, showing a picture of the coronary arteries of the heart. I pointed out the area of concern as depicted by the stress study. I then discussed the reason for needing to know whether what was seen on the noninvasive study, was correct. Both the patient and the wife were very appreciative of my taking time to explain the concern that existed with the one vessel of his heart. I recommended that he undergo the heart catheterization study to finalize whether or not the artery in question showed a critical lesion, and if so, what the definitive treatment should be. After I had made my last comment, the patient said, "Isn't it remarkable how God can bring two good people together like this?" I thanked the gentleman for his kind remark.

The above paragraph describes my usual approach to the caring of my patients. It requires a little extra time but none that is wasted. I could share story after story about the making of a physician. It never comes to an end until that last patient has been cared for. That last patient seen by me occurred on the last Tuesday afternoon of July 2015. My calling into medicine has been an exciting, adventurous journey—a continuum. I have now become a physician. I am grateful I chose that lesser path to be traveled. Below the reader will find two notes from the employees of the Ohio State University Heart Clinic of Cambridge, Ohio. Following that, the reader will also find a tear-jerking commendation from the Ohio State House of Representatives. Both are received with immense humility.

Happy + ! ☺
golfing +
gardening! Thank you, Julie

Happy Retirement!
It's been a Pleasure
working with you!
thank you!! Brenda.

Happy Retirement!!!
Again.

Dr. Graber! Kim
I am going to
miss you terrible.
Respectfully,
Christina

Dr. Graber,
You have been such a positive influence in what can be a very negative world. Thank you for being such an inspiration. Enjoy retirement + your family. You will be missed. Sharon

Dr. Graber,
It has been a pleasure working with you. You have been an inspiration + asset to our community. You are one of a kind. You will be missed here at our office. Best of luck!

Rusty

P.S. You can always comeback.
☺

We thank you <u>so</u> much
for your time here @ Cambridge
Heart. It has been a true
pleasure working with you. You
have made a difference in
our office and the lives of
the patients you treated. May
each day of your re-retirement
be enjoyable! Best wishes!!

Dr. Shaber,

Saying goodbye has never been easy for me, especially when I became attach to someone. You are the epitome of a gentle and caring doctor. As my Grandmother would say, they broke the mold when you were born. I want to thank you from the bottom of my heart for giving your time to us for the last 9 months. You did make a difference and you will be sadly missed by everyone. In my 23 years being in the medical field I had never met or probabley will never meet another doctor like you. You have been my hero, mentor and inspiration. Enjoy retirement (again) and remember us, because I will always remember you.

Respectfully,
AnnMarie

UNDER THE SPONSORSHIP OF

REPRESENTATIVE DOROTHY PELANDA
HOUSE DISTRICT 83

On behalf of the members of the House of Representatives of the 129th General Assembly of Ohio, we are pleased to extend special recognition to

DR. HARRY GRABER

for your outstanding work as a doctor.

Throughout fifty years of distinguished service in the field of medicine, you have demonstrated an unwavering dedication to performing your duties and fulfilling your responsibilities with the utmost efficiency and competence. The first director of Mary Rutan Hospital, a doctor with Oak Hill Medical Practice and Cardiology Associates of Bellefontaine, and an instructor at The Ohio State University School of Medicine, you have striven to better the world around you, and your tireless efforts have been truly inspirational. Always sincere and energetic in your approach to your work, you have given freely of your time and abilities far beyond what was required or expected and have displayed a genuine commitment to attaining your goals in a skillful and professional manner.

The enthusiasm and generosity you have shown in all of your endeavors have earned you the gratitude and respect of the patients and their families that you have so capably served. As you reflect on your career, you have the satisfaction of knowing that you have provided a vital service to the community, helping innumerable people to achieve optimum health, and have established a record of personal and professional accomplishment that will stand as a hallmark for others to emulate.

Thus, with great pleasure, we commend you for your exemplary work and salute you as one of Ohio's finest citizens.

Representative Dorothy Pelanda
House District 83

WILLIAM G. BATCHELDER
SPEAKER
OHIO HOUSE OF REPRESENTATIVES

CHAPTER 14

Curricula Vitae:

Graduated from Leo High School (1949)

BS in Education from Goshen College (1954)

Doctor of Medicine, St. Louis University (1964)

Specialty in Internal Medicine, Akron, Ohio (1969)

Internal Medicine Medical Boards (1970)

Founder, Mary Rutan Hospital Cardiology Department (1978)

West Liberty-Salem School Board of Education (late 1970s to early 1980s)

Postgraduate training (Cardiology Fellow), Ohio State University (2.5 years) (1974–1979)

American College of Cardiology Fellow (1989)

Assistant clinical professor of medicine, Ohio State University (1989–2012); emeritus status (2012–present)

Medical director, Mary Rutan Hospital (1990–1999)

Logan County Health Board (1992–2007)

Commendation from JACHO, representing the highest award a hospital can receive (October 1990)

Distinguished Service Award—for founding, development, and twenty-year growth of cardiology department at Mary Rutan Hospital (July 1991)

Mary Rutan Hospital Meritorious Award (March 1992)

Bellefontaine Kiwanis Citizen of the Year Award (February 1997)

CHAPTER 15

Other Selected Comments About the Author

Dr. Graber is a unique individual with outstanding interpersonal and clinical skills. He was primarily responsible for leading the city of Bellefontaine into state-of-the-art cardiology care. He, with Dr. Evan Dixon and Dr. Vincent Petno, brought cardiac diagnosis and therapy to a prime level when such was available primarily at the large medical or major city hospital. Dr. Graber had been well trained and then took additional cardiology training in echocardiography, nuclear medicine, and pacemaker insertion and technology so that all these modalities were available at the Mary Rutan Hospital. He was instrumental in obtaining the hospital's support for equipment and facilities to provide first-rate care at the local facility. While his leadership was so important to the development of outstanding cardiac care locally, the patients who were fortunate to receive the evaluations and care would speak to Dr. Graber's personal attributes. Dr. Graber was always forthright, humble, and able to communicate in a knowledgeable and caring fashion with those he had the opportunity to see as patients, peers, or hospital workers and administration personnel. His patients always spoke glowingly of his patience, care, and careful discussion of their illness, options, potential outcomes—and always with that personal insight into their lives which so importantly melded their decisions. Dr. Graber was clearly a great leader and communicator who furthered greatly the medical and cardiology care in Central Ohio.

Stephan Schaal, MD, FACC
Professor Emeritus of Internal Medicine
and Cardiovascular Disease
Director of Electrophysiology Laboratory (1972–1994)
Ohio State University Medical Center

***

Dr. Harry Graber, a venerable colleague, assembled this work on physicians' testimonial regarding their career choices. Having served as the sole cardiologist for the community of Bellefontaine, Ohio, for decades, Dr. Graber was recruited into the faculty ranks of the Ohio State University Cardiology Division for his talents and skill as a superb diagnostician and model physician. As a practicing physician, he became the principal investigator (and provided more than 95 percent of the clinical care of the large Ohio State family of inherited cardiomyopathy (*Circulation* 74 (1986), 21–35). This book highlights one of Dr. Graber's deep interests: what makes physicians tick and perform the way they do. You will be fascinated by the vignettes and life experiences.

Carl Leier, MD, FACC
Professor Emeritus of Internal Medicine
and Cardiovascular Disease
and Director of the Division of Cardiology
Ohio State University Medical Center (1986–1998)

CHAPTER 16

Summary

Both *genetic* and *environmental* factors play important roles in one's life. Genetics remains a fixed entity whereas environment is a variable. Environmental experiences in life can have a positive or negative influence upon the genetic makeup of a given individual. Decision-making in the preschool environment is predominantly controlled by parents. Eventually, the individual being influenced by the many past environmental factors becomes the responsible "choice maker" as to which path in life he/she wishes to travel. It is my belief that it is *providential* that one is given these experiences to aid in our decision-making. This concept was supported by five of the physicians who shared their stories in (chapter 10). All were greatly influenced by *role model* individuals whom they encountered in their earlier life. This *influence factor* is not a single event but a continuum. This forms the basis of the concept that the making of a physician is not a one-time event but represents a *continuum*. For some of us, becoming a physician is understood as a calling.

The stories in this book were shared so that others may develop a greater appreciation of their own environmental experiences and consider them as influential factors in making decisions in their lives. It is also my hope that this book might be of positive help to the young person considering the medical profession as his or her vocation.

Harry L. Graber, MD, FACC
Assistant Clinical Professor of Medicine, Emeritus
Ohio State University School of Medicine
Division of Cardiology

BIBLIOGRAPHY:

1. Bhattacharjee, Yudhijit. *National Geographic* January 2015, 58–79.
2. Whitman, Walt. There was a child went forth. *Oxford Book of American Verse*, 1950.
3. Frost, Robert. The road not taken. *Oxford Book of American Verse*, 1950.
4. Hukel, Jean. *The Graber Family*. Couthenans, France, 1984.
5. U.S. 66. Wikipedia.
6. Population and Size of Navajo Nation. Wikipedia.
7. Assistant Dean of St. Louis School of Medicine. Hippocratic Oath. St. Louis Guild of the Catholic Church.
8. Mary Rutan Hospital Administration. Early History and Current Operations of Mary Rutan Hospital. 2016.
9. Wooley, Lucia; Christofer; Steve. Early history of husband and father. 2016.
10. Wooley, Christofer. The bigger picture. Unpublished manuscript
11. Rick, Pauline. Mercy Ships: History of Mercy Ship Ministry. 2016

ABOUT THE AUTHOR:

Harry L. Graber, M.D. was born and raised on a farm in northeastern Indiana on August 23, 1931. He was a non-thriving infant for the first two years of life. Like most families, they were poor and learned to live without luxuries. The principle of work before play was well understood. Like his father, he was destined to become a farmer, but at age 14 he developed a critical illness. The physician stated, "Unless God intervened, he was not expected to live." Three weeks later he was on his way to recovery. After completing high school he entered college, majoring in education. During his third year of college, his favorite professor said, "I think God has something else for you, other than becoming a teacher." After graduation he taught school on the Navajo Reservation in Arizona. While there he perceived a calling to enter the medical profession. He is a graduate of St. Louis University School of Medicine and spent his career in cardiology at Mary Rutan Hospital of Bellefontaine, Ohio and Ohio State University.